Elevate
Copyright © 2022 by Rose Buttercup Publishing
ISBN: 978-0-6489476-7-7

All rights reserved. No portion of this book may be reproduced mechanically, electronically, or by any other means, including photocopying, without permission of the publisher or author except in the case of brief quotations embodied in critical articles and reviews. It is illegal to copy this book, post it to a website, or distribute it by any other means without permission from
the publisher or author.

Limits of Liability and Disclaimer of Warranty-
The author and publisher shall not be liable for your misuse of the enclosed material. This book is strictly for informational and educational purposes only.

Disclaimer-
The purpose of this book is to educate and entertain. The author and/or publisher do not guarantee that anyone following these techniques, suggestions, tips, ideas, or strategies will become successful. The author and/or publisher shall have neither liability nor responsibility to anyone with respect to any loss or damage caused, or alleged to be caused, directly or indirectly by the information contained in this book.

Medical Disclaimer-
The medical or health information in this book is provided as an information resource only, and is not to be used or relied on for any diagnostic or treatment purposes. This information is not intended to be patient education, does not create any patient-physician relationship, and should not be used as a substitute for professional diagnosis and treatment.

First Printing, 2022

ELEVATE

ELEVATE

THE PRACTICAL GUIDE TO LIVING YOUR BEST LIFE & SUCCEEDING

FILIZ BEHAETTIN

Post pictures or quotes related to this book on social media using the tag **#ElevateBook** so we can like and feature them on our page

To my parents and brother, for always supporting me.
-xox-

Contents

Dedication — vi

Preface — 1

Introduction — 4

1. Embracing failure & negative emotions to succeed — 7
2. Find your purpose — 13
3. Conquer your mindset — 19
4. Success comes to those who believe it — 26
5. A strong faith — 31
6. Perseverance is key — 36
7. Circumstances mean nothing — 41
8. Create your own habits & routine — 46
9. The art of saying 'no' — 50
10. Find your balance — 58
11. Let relationships be easy — 63

12	Let go of fear	69
13	Procrastination is a vibe killer	74
14	Be willing to be imperfect	80
15	Be your own agent	87
16	The making of choices	93
17	Visualise your way to success	98
18	Be open to receiving & prosper	104
19	The power of healing	110

Epilogue	116
Acknowledgements	119
Index	121
About The Author	126

Preface

The sun rises over Melbourne, its rays glistening off the water as I sit on the beach to write this preface. It's a beautiful morning in a place known for its unpredictable weather and multiple seasons in one day, but I wouldn't trade it for anything. Melbourne is the city I was born and raised in, where I call home, and where my family emigrated to after the war in Cyprus. I sit on the same beach I spent most of my childhood building sandcastles, collecting seashells, and frolicking in the sun. It is no coincidence that I have chosen this particular location to write the preface to my first self-help book. This special place fills my soul with happiness, but today, my heart is even more full, knowing the valuable information you will receive from reading my book – *Elevate*

Elevate is precisely that, a book about elevating you to greater heights in life while teaching you how to receive all that you seek in this life, experiencing fulfilment as you move through the different phases of your life.

No matter where you are in life, what you are dealing with, however big or small, life can always get better if you are willing to open yourself to a new way of doing things and thinking. This book provides easy yet practical exercises and tools to open your mind to new possibilities and shift your life to one of fulfilment and joy. I would recommend you read the whole book before you begin to work on the exercises found in this book. Through consistent use, you will be able to bring yourself to experience more abundance, happiness, and prosperity.

Life is supposed to be enjoyed and bring us harmony, yet so many people sadly go through life living in despair and misery. This is because they fail to see the endless opportunities available to them and, by doing so, attract to them more of what they do not want.

The purpose of writing this book was to give you the tools you need to succeed, empower, and show you that you possess the magnificent power to change any circumstance in your life. I would know, as I've used the same techniques I mention in this book, to bring my dreams into reality and experience the beautiful gifts that come with this.

As you read this book, you will also see how connecting and aligning with your greater purpose in life and higher self will open the door to things you would have once thought impossible.

There is a reason you were drawn to this book, as nothing is of coincidence in this life. Somewhere in the pages of this book may hide the answer to a question you once asked or sought. Whatever the reason, I am incredibly grateful to be able to accompany and guide you on your new path to fulfilment.

With love and light,

Filiz

Introduction

Are you sick of constantly facing roadblocks to your path to success, or perhaps you are looking for something new in life, more fulfilling, or simply want to improve your current life circumstances?

We were all put on this world to achieve greatness, and you are no exception to this.

Regardless of what is currently happening in your life, you can achieve and be all you want while living and experiencing a fulfilling life. But before we send you off and hand you the keys to unlocking your true potential, you must have a clear understanding of your inner being.

There are two sides to a person, one being the physical, what you see when you look in the mirror, and the other, is the energy you radiate. Those unfamiliar with the latter will see themselves as physical beings and nothing else, but we all vibrate with energy, even those who have crossed over.

The energy a person carries will always be pure in nature. However, their feelings, behaviour, and decisions will always mould their energy to either work for or against them. Some people can be their own worst enemies, but it does not have to be this way.

Throughout this book, you will learn how to use practical skills you can apply in your everyday life to bring to fruition whatever you desire by being aware of your vibrational frequencies.

We all have an infinite supply of capabilities as we are all vibrational beings; however, your lack of conscious awareness prevents you from releasing the marvellous power you have within. Once you become consciously aware of your thoughts, intentions, fears, and self-limiting beliefs, you will be able to transition and shift to a world where you begin to receive the things that once upon a time seemed out of reach.

These concepts we have spoken about may appear unfamiliar to you, but do not worry. As you move through the book's various chapters, you will see first-hand how applying the concepts outlined in this book will assist you in living a rewarding and satisfying life. While overcoming the things that had once upon a time prevented you from achieving the greatness you seek.

As you become more aware of the power of your consciousness, you will find that your inner and outer perceptions of the world and the opinions you carry will begin to change. You will also find yourself becoming more understanding and compassionate towards others, as they will with you. Furthermore, you will also start attracting like-minded individuals operating on the same vibrational frequencies as you.

The moment you become conscious of your inner being and its connection to your physical world, you begin to encounter people and experiences that bring you joy and help you connect to your definite purpose in life.

A person must have a definite purpose in life to achieve their desired success. As this is a crucial element to success, we have dedicated an entire chapter to this topic which you will find as you read along. In addition, this chapter is equipped with easy-to-use practical exercises to assist you in identifying your purpose, should you not know what that is.

From a young age, I have always known I wanted to be a writer, yet, as I transitioned to adulthood, like many other individuals, I began working in the corporate world. However, my passion for writing never dwindled, so I started a new chapter in my own life when I entered the writing world with the release of my children's series and became a published author.

As my writing journey evolved, so did my life; doors opened that I could only have once dreamed of, but that wasn't the only thing that happened. All of a sudden, I became acquainted with individuals I had admired growing up and connected to people from all over the world.

The alignment of my inner being with my purpose increased the feeling of balance and harmony in my life and brought me great joy. So likewise, when you align with your inner being and higher self, everything in your life will also come into alignment and bring you more success, fulfilment, and happiness than you've ever experienced.

I am by no means here to tell you how to live your life, but I am here through this book to assist and empower you in being the best version of yourself and equipping you with the tools you need to succeed in whatever it is you desire.

Now let us begin –

I

Embracing failure & negative emotions to succeed

Introducing a self-help book with the topic of failure may seem strange, but it is one of the most common themes overlooked when discussing success and the tools required to live your best life. Many believe that failure is horrible and frightening when it can be one of the most beneficial things to happen to a person at times. You see, failure and success go hand in hand.

Failure is merely a simple way of informing the individual that their actions are not working and that an alternative route is needed to reach their desired destination. Think of the GPS in your car; what happens when you miss a turn? It likely starts reprogramming itself, finding an alternative route to reach your desired destination. The same principles apply to failure. Failure is your very own personalised GPS that eventually guides you to your desired destination – *if you let it!*

We say if you let it because, sadly, most individuals who meet with defeat are quick to give up on their goals and dreams instead of looking for an alternative way to get there. When an individual fails time and time again, it is not because they are *'failures.'* Rather, it is the programming of their mind that continues to deliver the same unwanted results to them. We will delve into this topic in more detail in the coming chapters; however, it is worth noting that the word *'failure'* is not bad, nor should you fear it. Failure is part of everyone's journey and does not discriminate. Whether you are the president of a country, a CEO, unemployed, or working a corporate job, failure affects everyone at one time or another in their lives. Nonetheless, there is a fine line between succeeding and continually failing, separating the fortunate from the unfortunate.

> *"FORTUNATE ARE THE ONES WHO HAVE MASTERED THEIR MIND AND BELIEF SYSTEM; UNFORTUNATE ARE THE ONES WHO ARE YET TO REALISE THE GREAT POTENTIAL LYING WITHIN THEMSELVES."*

The fortunate embrace their failures, while the others sadly choose to flounder in them. This is not to say that the fortunate are in any way better than the unfortunate, but rather that the fortunate have mastered and created healthy habits when dealing with defeat and trying times.

One of the many issues facing those who fail is that they permit their identity to become intertwined with their level of success. Individuals who share this thinking will always perceive themselves as *'failures'* when they meet defeat instead of seeing it as an opportunity to grow and find improved methods to get to where they wish to be. The best way for an individual to deal with failure is to embrace it, which involves acknowledging the negative emotions they feel and letting those emotions flow freely through them. The first reaction of some individuals is to dismiss the negative emotions they feel and act as if they are irrelevant or void. Unfortunately, this does more harm than good, as the next time they deal with failure or an unwanted situation, the same negative emotions will most likely come to the surface. The long-term implications of this are even worse, with some individuals losing the complete ability to cope with unwanted situations healthily. At times and in rare instances, this can involve turning to substance abuse or other dangerous methods as a coping mechanism. Do not resign yourself to this kind of living or thinking; it is not only harmful but tiring. Instead, learn to accept and acknowledge failure and any negative emotions you feel, giving yourself permission to heal and move onto a new path.

Permission to heal is different from giving up. Permission to heal means you accept what you are feeling and understand that any defeat or failure you encounter is only temporary, guiding you to an alternative and improved path to that of success and fulfilment. Remember this point when dealing with failure and the emotions associated with it. No feeling or defeat is permanent; it is only permanent if you ALLOW it.

THE 48-HOUR RULE

If you are an individual who struggles with letting go of negative emotions, I recommend using the '48-hour' rule. As the title suggests, the 48-hour rule is the maximum period we enable for feelings of defeat and failure. This is also known as the 'mourning' period, in which you permit the negative emotions to flow freely through you during this time, and just as a snake sheds its skin to allow for further growth, you will shed yourself of the emotions that do not serve you once this time has elapsed. Setting a deadline for holding onto negative emotions makes it easier to transition to the letting go phase, which is vital when getting back on track to achieving one's goals and dreams. Individuals who stay in a negative mindset will only blur their vision and path to success, stopping them from reaching their full potential.

During the 'mourning' period, you will use a notepad to write down the reasons for the emotions you are feeling and the types of emotions you are having. For example, ask yourself the following questions:

- *What am I feeling?*
- *Why am I feeling the way I am?*
- *Am I sad, angry, or disappointed? What are the exact emotions I am feeling?*
- *Does failure define who I am? If so, why do I enable the failure to define me?*

It is important you follow these instructions down to a tee if you want to see any progress in your life and achieve your dreams. In addition, during the 'mourning' period, it is required you write down and say the following affirmation out loud two times a day:

> *"I permit myself to heal and know that I am not defeated but rather growing in strength."*

After the end of the two days, you will take the answers you have written down to the above questions and tear the paper apart as a physical sign of letting go of the emotions that do not serve your higher self. This will act as an indicator to your subconscious mind that you are ready to discover a new path to reach the destination you seek. Alternatively, some individuals prefer burning their written answers to indicate the beginning of their new path. Whichever method speaks to you and your soul is the best one to use. If you do choose the second method, please always exercise caution and safety when doing so. The more you practise the 48-hour rule, the easier it will be to rid yourself of negative emotions. If you practise it long enough, you will become so in tune with your feelings and letting go of what no longer serves you that you will not even need to practise the 48-hour rule anymore, nor will you fear failure but rather accept it as a part of your journey.

Failure should never be looked at as something that is final or the end all be all. Failure, like all things in life, is only temporary. The more you understand this; the more harmonious your life will be.

There is no doubt in life you will experience failure in a number of different ways, but with each failure comes a beautiful lesson. How you react to these failures and the lessons learned will make you succeed or perish. Know this and embrace the philosophy presented, and you will already have a much more in-depth understanding than the majority of individuals you are surrounded by or know. Ironically, many individuals claim to understand this philosophy. But instead, their actions and results say otherwise. Even the great Sir Edmund Hillary, who climbed Mt Everest failed numerous times before achieving what no man before him did. Yet, had he given up the first time he met with defeat, he would not have achieved the remarkable feat that he did.

Failure is a blessing, and as you delve deeper into this book, you will see how failure and the other principles discussed will come together, enabling you to succeed and live a much more rewarding and harmonious life.

2

Find your purpose

Life is miraculous, but what makes it even more remarkable is that only one of you is in this world. Each of us has the capabilities to do whatever we desire. But unfortunately, while we live in an era where anything is possible, many people go through life doubting their abilities and ruining their chance at success even before they begin. One of the reasons for this is that they lack direction and have not yet come to understand their definite purpose in life. So instead, they travel through life in a mediocre way, not knowing they can experience the life of their dreams if they choose.

> *"IF ONE WANTS TO SUCCEED AND LIVE A FULFILLED LIFE, THEN ONE MUST IDENTIFY THEIR PURPOSE AND COMMIT TO IT."*

Whether we are aware of it or not, all of us have a purpose in this life. Your purpose is why you do what you do and what brings you continued fulfilment and satisfaction in life. It is the feeling of being inspired each morning you get up and before you go to bed. It is having the knowledge that what you do in life makes a change or impacts someone somewhere in this world. Yet, there is a common misconception amongst most people who identify earning money as their definite purpose in life. While money is part of our lives, it is merely a transaction that results from exchanging a service or item for payment. Of course, everyone desires to have more money, but that is not your definite purpose in life.

Your definite purpose in life is one which brings you riches and abundance in ALL areas of your life, not just specific areas like your finances. A person who has found their true purpose, will be one who experiences fulfilment and joy in everything they do along with those closest to them. On the other hand, there are people who receive such monetary gain and success yet will suffer from ongoing negative experiences such as bad health or problematic marriages and relationships with their children because they have either not come into alignment with their purpose or do not know what it is. Whatever the reason, it is safe to say purpose and fulfilment will always bind one's success with riches in all areas of their life. This is why we have strongly emphasised the correlation between finding your purpose and the amount of fulfilment you will feel. If one does not feel pure ecstasy when associating with their purpose, then it is safe to say they have not found their true-life purpose.

To assist you in beginning the process of identifying your purpose, ask yourself the following questions:

- *What is it that I truly desire to be and do?*
- *What do I want my legacy to be?*
- *What brings me the most joy in life?*
- *What are my burning passions?*
- *What strengths have assisted me in overcoming the obstacles of my life?*
- *How have my strengths helped others, including my friends and family, when dealing with difficulties in their lives?*

Some individuals may be able to answer these questions straight away, while others may need a bit more time. We recommend asking yourselves these questions once a week for four weeks. This is because the more you do it, the more detailed your answers will become. Once you complete the four weeks, you will collate all your responses and look for common themes and characteristics among them. This will guide you in finding your purpose and niche and any core values that align with your higher self and bring you fulfilment.

Having a definite purpose is not only the pathway to living your dream life but also the secret link to developing your creative imagination and improving one's zest for life and self-discipline. While each component has a place in turning the wheels of your intention and purpose into motion, imagination is the most crucial of the elements.

CREATIVE IMAGINATION

An individual's creative imagination is not only a magnificent and powerful tool but also one of the most valuable tools available to them. It is where all our greatest desires and ideas take shape. The most incredible gadgets in the world first came to life through the imagination, even the chair you are sitting on; that was nothing but a desire that began to take shape in the imaginative mind. When the Wright brothers first decided they wanted to fly, that too was nothing but a burning desire, brought to life by none other than the creative imagination.

The creative imagination with a definite purpose can make the impossible possible. More importantly, it is available to everyone. There is no cost to using your imagination. It is a faculty that is readily accessible free of charge. However, without a definite purpose, it will not operate at the level of greatness that it can. Do not mistake this statement for saying there is no such thing as imagination without a definite purpose. Imagination exists within all of us. However, those who do not use their imagination will find they are limited in their abilities to reach their goals and succeed.

Those who claim they have *no imagination* have simply not yet adequately developed their imagination. If you, too, are one of those individuals who make such claims, I would suggest you work on strengthening this fantastic faculty that is known as *imagination* through your daily tasks. Look for and create new ways of carrying out your daily tasks more efficiently, whatever that may be. It would be best if you carried out this exercise independently and did not seek guidance from others. Your job is to strengthen your imaginative mind, and only you and you alone can do this. If you rely on others to find a solution to carry out your tasks efficiently, then you will not be able to develop your imagination in the manner that will bring you the success you so very much desire.

As children, we never question our creative imagination. The ideas it generates are accepted and believed by us. This is because the belief in our imagination and the ideas it develops during those stages of our young lives is so strong that we never question their actuality. Nothing is too far-fetched or out of reach at that age. But unfortunately, as we get older, most of us let the magical gift of our imaginations run away. Instead, we permit logic, circumstances, and feelings of misery and self-doubt to take over, leading to most individuals taking their first steps to a life of ordinariness.

Fortunately for me, being a writer, my creative imagination never entirely left my side, even as I transitioned into adulthood. I would often use my daily commute to work to come up with various stories and ideas or simply dream of the type of future I wanted to have. Sadly, this is not the case for most people, but thankfully, as you are reading this book, you are now aware of the importance of the creative imagination and will leverage its use more often to achieve all that you seek.

Permit the power of your imagination and definite purpose to guide you to a life filled with fulfilment and not one of dreariness. Allow your creative imagination to be the architect of your most outstanding achievements and dreams. Never underestimate its power. The magnitude of one's creative imagination and what it can bring into form is of such greatness; there are not enough words to capture the true essence of this fantastic gift. The universe has an abundant supply of tools available to us to achieve all that we desire in life, but it is up to us to take those tools and make the most of them.

3

Conquer your mindset

Purpose alone will not bring an individual the success or abundance they desire if one does not learn how to conquer their mindset and self-limiting beliefs. How many times have you come across an individual who, no matter what they do or how hard they try, cannot achieve the goals they set themselves? There is nothing wrong with the individual in question; rather, the barriers they have placed upon their mind prevent them from achieving what they desire. Unfortunately, at times, an individual may not even know they have deep-rooted barriers which are impacting their results. Before we delve deeper into how we can overcome the barriers we place upon ourselves, it is important we have a good understanding of the relationship between our thoughts and belief system. Thoughts and ideas alone do not make an individual stay in a negative mindset; instead, the intense emotion we associate with these negative thoughts and ideas keeps us in a state of misery. When we associate strong emotions with a thought or idea, it becomes a belief in our subconscious mind. This controls how we react and act in various situations.

SELF-EVALUATION & THE SUBCONSCIOUS MIND

The subconscious mind is our operating system and the key to our success and failures. It does not know the difference between a good or bad thought. It simply takes whatever thought you are feeding it and brings it into form. If you continually saturate your subconscious mind with negative thoughts or self-limiting beliefs, it will continue to bring you the opposite of what you desire. Whatever we give attention to, the subconscious mind magnifies.

An individual must also understand that you can desire something with your conscious mind. However, if you do not truly believe you will achieve it in your subconscious mind, you will fail to bring your desire to fruition.

So, how can one get rid of self-limiting beliefs and their barriers?

Through self-evaluation.

If you make a committed decision to live a life filled with purpose and the abundance you desire, then it is equally important you make the decision to self-evaluate. This requires one to go deep within themselves and address any negative beliefs one may associate with themselves. To begin your self-evaluation process, take a notebook and write down all the areas in life you are failing in. This can be anything from your career to your relationships. Next, study your list, and then taking a separate piece of paper, draw a line down the middle so you have two columns. First, write down why you believe you are failing in the left-hand column. Next, write down the exact opposite of your negative statement in the right-hand column. We are doing this exercise to help you understand the negative beliefs you have been feeding your subconscious mind so you can reprogram them. Only when you change your belief system can you begin to see a shift in your physical life.

Now, let us continue.

Upon completing this task, create a small summary of your positive statements, carefully including all the key points you have highlighted to produce one positive statement overall. This one positive statement can be as long or short as you wish. You will then need to write out your positive statement at least 10x per day for a minimum of 90 days. While this may seem excessive, the power of repetition is needed if you are to shift and change your self-limiting beliefs.

POWER OF REPETITION – WHY YOU NEED IT

As mentioned earlier, your operating system doesn't know the difference between good and bad thoughts. It takes whatever thought you continuously have and brings it into form. By exercising repetition, you are changing what you are feeding your operating system into what you desire rather than what you don't want or have.

A lot of individuals exercise the power of repetition for a few days or weeks and then say it doesn't work. However, you must understand that repetition is not something you can do for a short period. Instead, it is something you need to commit to doing for an extended time as it will bring you closer to your end goal and enable you to better deal with your negative thoughts. This is because you will find yourself making a conscious approach to saturate your mind with only the thoughts and ideas that serve you and your purpose, rather than the ones that limit your ability to achieve what you desire. The more you exercise, the power of repetition, the more it will come naturally to you.

For example, if a person constantly says, *"I never have enough money,"* they never will. This is not because they want to struggle but rather because they are focusing on their 'lack' of money and consequently permitting that to be their dominating thought. A person must understand that to achieve and reach their desired success; they must be wary of the dominating thoughts they keep. It would be best to have positive thoughts, believe what you affirm just as you believe, and know that night follows day. Only then will you see a shift in your life, bring what you desire into reality, and connect to your higher self.

ACTING AS IF

Another crucial element a person must learn to receive and achieve what they desire is the principle of *'acting as if,'* which entails a person *'living in the end.'* Simply put, this concept involves individuals acting as if they have already acquired whatever it is they seek or desire. It is a straightforward enough concept, yet one that a lot of people struggle to grasp and understand, mainly because they cannot get into the vibration of feeling the emotions that one would if they had what it is they desire to have.

Individuals can believe they have something, but if they do not actually feel the deep, intense emotion associated with possessing what they desire, they will struggle with bringing it to fruition. Therefore, individuals must ask themselves, *"If I had what I desired, how would I feel? Would I be excited, content, or happy? What would I do, be or act like?"*

Regardless of what you desire, you must get into the vibrational state of the emotions associated with it to receive it. Receiving what you want starts with making a committed decision that you will have what you desire and then acting as if you already have it. You need not focus on the process of how you will acquire what it is you desire, as the 'how' will come later.

Now, let us say your greatest desire is to own a sizable ten-bedroom property or luxury vehicle, but you currently own an average-looking vehicle and live in an old, cramped apartment. Of course, your reality is far from what you desire, but that doesn't mean you can't 'act as if.' To get in touch with the deep emotions of owning that luxury vehicle, you can take yourself to your local luxury car dealership and sit in your choice of car, smell the leather seats, take it for a test drive, or pretend when driving your old car, that you are in fact driving the car of your dreams. The same goes for the luxury home you desire. Visit the luxury homes they have for sale, walk around the house, sit at the dining table and visualise yourself enjoying dinner or celebrating a birthday with your loved ones in your new spacious home. If you can't go out in person and do that, take virtual tours online and feel the intense emotions associated with having what you desire. What you desire must be felt first in order to become real.

I knew a lady who used the same principles explained to get herself out of debt. Instead of focusing on the negative emotions of being in debt, each time she received a bill or notice with an amount owing, she would simply say, *"I am so grateful and thankful to be receiving this cheque of x amount. My bank account is continually growing."* After a few months of doing this, she received a cheque with a substantial amount owed to her from a previous client. This helped her clear her debts, enabled her to invest in herself and cleared the way for a more abundant-filled lifestyle.

While she might have been in debt at the time, her physical reality meant nothing to her. Instead, in her mind, she lived as if she had an abundant supply of income and associated with the positive feelings of being in abundance and living in prosperity. Sure enough, eventually, her physical reality reflected this.

So, when we say the feeling of possessing what you desire is critical, we mean it.

As mentioned in the previous chapters, your operating system does not know the difference between a good or bad thought. It takes whatever you feed it and brings it into form. It would have been easy for the lady in question to wallow in her debts or continually feel sorry for herself, but she chose to live in the end and changed things for herself.

Long before I owned the luxury vehicle I currently drive, I decided that I would own and drive that specific brand and type of vehicle. I didn't question whether I could afford it or not or the how. I simply knew I would own that specific vehicle brand, and guess what? In a matter of months, I was driving the luxury vehicle of my choice and dreams.

When a person does not have any feelings of resistance to what they seek and associates with the positive high-vibrational feelings related to whatever they desire, their desire has no choice but to come into form through their physical world.

To the average person, the dream life they seek may appear out of reach, but you are not an average person. You are a vibrational being with an awareness of one's higher self and understand that nothing is out of reach when correctly using the principles discussed here.

4

Success comes to those who believe it

Each person has their own definition of success. To some, it may be having an extensive property portfolio, and to another, it may be working at a highly reputable organisation with a six-figure salary. Whatever success may look like to you, one must understand what one desires they can achieve. The belief system one holds is what makes a difference between succeeding and failing. An individual with a weak belief system will always choose to stay in a state of misery when dealing with failure, while the one with a success mindset will always get up and try again. The great Thomas Edison is the perfect example of an individual with a success mindset. He failed numerous times before finally reaching his goal. However, if he had chosen to give up and wallow in his many failed attempts, he would not have been able to bring his idea to fruition. Edison decided he would achieve what he set out to do, regardless of how long it would take him. He made a committed decision to succeed. He believed in his abilities and did not let his past results deter him from his end goal. Individuals who believe in their ability to get what they desire and do not let their past or present results dictate them will always succeed. *Success will always come to those who believe it.*

Since childhood, individuals have learned to associate failure with negative emotions rather than look at it as a potential opportunity for growing and learning. At school, individuals acquired the habit of letting report cards determine their level of success and failure. If one were to receive straight A's, the teachers would say their future looked bright and promising. Those who received anything below that, particularly those who received an F on their report card, would be considered incompetent individuals, destined to fail in various areas of their lives. Yet, the world is full of high-school dropouts who have created multi-million-dollar business empires. While it is safe to say that a report card is not a reliable source to measure one's success, many individuals still carry these old-style beliefs well into adulthood. The main reason for this is that we continue to encounter similar reporting systems as we transition into adulthood and enter the workforce. There is no workforce that doesn't use KPIs, sales data, or other measures to determine one's value within an organisation. The issue with this is that many individuals use this same thinking process to decide whether or not they are a success or a failure, impacting their self-image in the long run.

An individual's belief system and self-image work together; however, whether they work positively or negatively depends on the individual. For example, a person will always succeed if they have a strong self-image and belief system. On the other hand, if a person suffers from a negative self-image, they will struggle to operate at their full potential and reach their goals. There can be several reasons why a person may have a negative self-image. But more often than not, it stems from an individual's childhood and experience and the outdated reporting systems used in schools and organisations to determine their value. Another fatal and common dominator that impacts one's perception of themselves is the opinions others hold of them. An individual who is constantly belittled by their peers or those closest to them will eventually take on the negative thoughts they have been projected to over time unless they have a strong mindset.

BELIEVE IN YOU

Our outer reality is always a reflection of the emotions and thoughts we hold on the inside. If an individual constantly takes on the negative thoughts and opinions others have of them; they will eventually develop a negative self-image. If you are guilty of this, and many individuals are, stop it now! Learn to love yourself and let go of the opinions others have of you. An individual who loves themself will always be one who wins. Unfortunately, there is a misconception that loving yourself is somewhat shallow or egotistic, which is not the case. The time has come for individuals to rid themselves of such thoughts and beliefs and learn that a loving and healthy relationship with themselves is a prerequisite to having a positive belief system that encourages success and fulfilment. Loving yourself means being happy with 'you' as a whole, not the 'you' others love about you, but the *'you'* that makes you *'you.'* You are an infinite being with an infinite source of potential. There is only one of you in a world filled with approximately 7.9 billion people. Thus, you are a uniquely gifted being who is capable of achieving great things if you believe in yourself!

When you get up in the morning and look in the mirror, affirm the following:

"I am worthy of love, money & happiness."

This particular affirmation is to help guide and shift you towards a positive self-image filled with love and prosperity. A strong self-image will also provide you with the self-confidence you need to obtain whatever you desire in life. Self-confidence does not involve one thinking they are better than the next person or belittling people. Instead, when used correctly, self-confidence means trusting in one's capabilities and believing one can do whatever their heart desires. Another part of self-confidence we should touch on is comparing oneself to others. Individuals with self-confidence do not compare themselves to others or associate with feelings of jealousy and hatred. If you are an individual who constantly compares yourself to others, you have not yet mastered self-confidence. Self-confidence means being truly comfortable in one's skin and trusting in the ability to achieve greatness. It also means one is open to learning from others, rather than associating with jealousy and hatred or other forms of ill and negative emotions detrimental to one's success and achievements. Genuinely self-confident individuals will surround themselves with fellow individuals who support and celebrate their wins, goals & losses. Aligning oneself with like-minded individuals prevents one from falling into the trap of their old toxic beliefs. If you truly want to shift to a life filled with prosperity, abundance, and one filled with fulfilment, let go of any toxicity surrounding you, including the individuals who bring you down. When you begin to exercise strong faith in your abilities to succeed and the self-confidence that reflects this, nothing can stop you from reaching the goals you previously thought were not possible.

5

A strong faith

Faith is the fertile garden of the mind. The same way you were to sow seeds in the ground and yield a grand harvest is the same way the roots of your greatest desires will cultivate when the time comes with the power of faith. It is a magical apparatus that will never let you down. It is of such a miraculous power that it defies all logic and science and transmutes one's greatest desires and dreams into physical reality. Remember, faith can only be called upon by an individual who has grasped all the concepts discussed in this book so far, and one who has conquered their mindset. Faith will always be a devoted servant of one's belief system that never makes an error in what it delivers to an individual in physical form. Failure to properly understand faith's true meaning and power will only give an individual more of what they do not want.

If you find that you are constantly receiving what you do not want, it is not faith that has failed you, but rather the negative thoughts you have enabled to enter and consume the mind. A weak belief system will always result in a weak faith. An individual who has lost their faith is one that will lose in life, but it need not be that way. Faith lives deep within all of us and is capable of being summoned upon command by letting go of all the negative thoughts in our belief system that do not serve us. Faith never disappears in the mind of a non-believer; it simply lays dormant, waiting to reappear when called upon.

BUILDING FAITH

The concept of faith is not something you can physically see, as it first must be felt by a person before it can bring one's greatest desires and achievements into the living and physical world. The miraculous thing about faith is that it is something that can be built or strengthened, even in the mind of a non-believer or during a time when one faces great adversity. However, a person's faith is not something that should only be utilised during challenging times, but at all times. Yet, we commonly observe that most individuals only attempt to rely on their faith in times of adversity.

The greatest supporter of having a strong faith is an individual's belief system, which is why to build or strengthen your faith, you should use the power of repetition and positive affirmations. Unfortunately, many individuals undervalue the power of using affirmations to achieve the greatness and success they desperately seek in their lives. Yet, it is common knowledge that affirmations are the only known way to create feelings of a strong faith in a person voluntarily. There are several reasons for this, but none should concern you as much as the beliefs you keep and have of yourself in your mind. You see, a person cannot utilise the power of faith to bring to fruition what they desire if they continually hold onto negative emotions and thoughts about themselves. Some of these negative emotions include feelings of greed, hatred, frustration, and jealousy. Thus, a good affirmation to use throughout the day to assist you in coming into a positive state and, therefore, improving and building your faith is:

> "It is my dominant intention that I only choose the feeling of joy today."

Joy is one of the most beautiful emotions a person can have and one that is available in abundance. Everywhere a person looks, they can find joy, provided they choose to see the beauty in the world. Joy can come in simple things, such as looking at a tree, the sound of the wind, raindrops, your pet, or anything else that makes you feel the intense emotion associated with joy and happiness. Joy is everywhere if you take the time to appreciate the greatness you are surrounded by. For example, as I woke and opened the blinds of my room in the early morning hours the other day, I met with the sight of two hot air balloons in the distance. I watched with such enthusiasm and joy till they were no longer visible to the naked eye. I pondered how magnificent it would be to have the opportunity to fly in one overlooking the Eiffel tower in Paris. Then my thoughts shifted to owning an apartment in Paris, which also brought me more happiness. None of these thoughts were negative, nor did I feel like they were out of reach. These thoughts simply brought me pure delight and put me in a higher vibrational state of receiving. What I was feeling was such positive emotion that as I moved through my workday, my mind filled with many more thoughts filled with joy, and by the time night came, I had such a glorious day I had no time to ponder on the little things that had not gone right during the day, nor did I care about it. What happened here was that I was in such a high vibrational frequency from the experience of the morning I permitted joy to be my only dominating emotion throughout my day. I chose to be in a state of bliss rather than one of negativity. It did not matter if the individuals around me were radiating negativity or negative things happened; what was important to me and my subconscious mind was that I was in a state of joy. That day as with all my days, I chose positive emotions and focused on taking steps to bring me closer to my ultimate goal. This only emphasised my strong faith and faith in my abilities to achieve what I set out to do.

A person's strong faith in their ability to succeed removes any self-limiting beliefs and negative emotions. It lets the individual know that any barriers they face on their journey to success will not be everlasting. Faith aids a person in getting closer to their greatest desires and brings endless opportunities for this to happen as each day passes. Furthermore, it assists the person in knowing that circumstances in their living and physical world, including the environment one is in, do not matter. This is something that everyone should be aware of, as individuals often tie their happiness to what is going on in their current physical circumstances or environment. They wait for their circumstances to change or hope to obtain something in their physical and living world before they can associate with the feelings of being happy and living a fulfilled life. These individuals almost always make comments such as: *"I'll feel happy when I have lots of money in my bank account,"* or *"I'll do this when the time is right."* This is an incorrect way of thinking. Before you can obtain what you so very much desire in life, you must first associate it with high feeling vibrations, such as joy, abundance, and happiness. You cannot get where you want when you feel lack or other low vibrational feelings such as doubt and fear. In fact, it is near impossible when a person is radiating such intense low vibrational thoughts or feelings. Of course, there will be rare instances where the circumstance of your physical world will be of such an extreme negative nature that you will struggle to radiate any positive high-flying emotions. In those rare instances, acknowledge what you are feeling and look for the tiniest thing that will bring you a hint of joy. This can be anything from staring at a flower to seeing a beautiful cloud in the sky, whatever it is; upon retreating to bed that night, remember that hint of happiness you felt earlier in the day. Slowly but surely, day by day, with your strong faith, you will begin to get back to feeling positive high-flying emotions, bringing you back to your path of success and fulfilment.

6

Perseverance is key

Perseverance. What a wonderful and underutilised thing it is. Perseverance combines the power of the will and faith, taking an individual to places they could only once dream upon. Look behind every successful person, and you will find perseverance lurking somewhere in the background. One can go as far back in history as they like, and they will see pages of books filled with stories of survival, conquering distant lands, or amazing inventions that would not have been possible without perseverance. These tales most often involve individuals from all walks of life, including soldiers, commoners, peasants, and even royalty. Not one individual who succeeded did not utilise the power of the will through perseverance. One of these individuals was Sultan Mehmed II also known as *'Mehmed the Conqueror'* of the Ottoman Empire, whose greatest conquest was seizing the great city of Constantinople in 1453, something his forefathers had tried but failed at succeeding. Sultan Mehmed II made it his life purpose to conquer the city of Constantinople, but what makes this conquest one worth mentioning is the perseverance and will that he displayed to reach his life purpose. To launch a successful siege, the Sultan and his soldiers would need to enter the 'Golden Horn,' a primary waterway and inlet of the Bosphorus. The issue with this was that the entrance to the 'Golden Horn' was blocked by huge chains, preventing unwanted ships from entering the waterway. With no way in, the Sultan needed to find an alternative route to enter the 'Golden Horn,' and here is where his power of perseverance and strong will to succeed came into play. The 'Golden Horn' was located near the well-known Galata bridge, which played a vital role in the Sultan's clever plan to enter the waterway. At the order of the Sultan, during nightfall, his soldiers removed their ships from the entrance of the Golden Horn where they were waiting and then rolled them through the land over the Galata, using nothing more than manual labour and some wooden logs. Once they safely made it through the Galata, the ships were placed back into the waterway, not outside the Golden Horn, *but inside it!* Something no one had previously thought of or done. Entering the Golden Horn was a vital strategic move in conquering Constantinople.

Sultan Mehmed II had a goal to succeed and conquer Constantinople, and that he did, using nothing but a strong will and perseverance. Of course, he faced a significant obstacle in his path to success, but that did not deter him. Instead, he focused on the end result and did what no one before him could do. Regardless of how big your dreams are or what you desire in life, and what your job title or status is, if one has a desire to succeed, one will. The sooner one understands this, the easier it is to accomplish one's goals. We all have the ability to do what we want in life; sadly, only a select few individuals actually understand this. It is natural for one to want to give up when defeat comes knocking at one's door, but do not let that phase you, for nothing is ever permanent in life. If one door doesn't open in time, you will find another one that will lead you to where you want to go. It really is as simple as that.

We saw in the example provided how Sultan Mehmed II defied logic and came up with an ingenious idea to enter the 'Golden Horn' by taking his ships out of the water and transporting them through the land. *What drove him to come up with such an idea?* It was nothing more than his will and strong belief in conquering Constantinople. Perseverance led Sultan Mehmed II to his success and cemented him as one of the greatest Sultans of that era. We speak of willpower and strong faith, as they are the building blocks of perseverance and what can bring one their most significant accomplishments in life. If you suffer from a lack of perseverance, it most likely stems from a low self-image and fear of others' criticism and judgement. It is rather sad, but unfortunately, it is all too common for individuals to permit others to think of how they should act or live their lives. These individuals most commonly come disguised as friends, family, or work colleagues. This results in the individual feeling 'obligated' to adhere to others' unrealistic expectations, making one fear judgement and criticism if one was to follow their dreams and goals. Then there are those who fear failure in general. These individuals choose the safety of familiarity instead of casting their nets far and wide into unknown waters. A lack of perseverance kills dreams and ambition before one even has time to bring their idea to life properly in their minds. If you want to build perseverance, you must have a burning desire to achieve your goal by believing in your purpose and knowing within the very depths of your soul that you will get to where you need to, regardless of the obstacles you may face in your path. Individuals who display perseverance have a solid ability to adjust and find alternative methods to reach their goals when something isn't working. Such individuals are also happy to associate themselves with like-minded individuals through mentoring, credibility groups, or confidantes to assist them in reaching their goals. Having a mentor or confidante can also enable individuals to share their thoughts without fearing being ridiculed by ordinary people. We say ordinary people not as an insult but as a way to show you there is still a lack of understanding amongst the general population of how one is a co-creator of their lives and a vibrational being and not merely just made up of flesh and bones. When like-minded individuals surround you, it is easier to stay on track to reach your goals and persevere in times of difficulty. It also enables one to keep negative thoughts and influences away.

What others think of one's goals and dreams will always be of least importance, but what one thinks of their own goals and dreams is what will enable one to persevere on their path to achievement and fulfilment. Always remember, a lack of ambition will always equate to a lack of perseverance. A lot of individuals who lack perseverance are forever making statements such as: *"I could never do that,"* or *"They're so successful, but I will never be as successful as them,"* and the best one of all,

"They have all the luck in the world." When one chooses to make such statements, they effectively say, "I do not have the capabilities to live the life I want because (insert excuse)." All these statements stem from one's negative thinking rather than learning to expect the results they seek. Individuals who succeed do not have more capabilities, skills, or opportunities than the next person. What they have are strong beliefs and the will to succeed. They believe that whatever obstacle one faces does not matter as they have the confidence and will to get to where they need to through perseverance.

It may appear odd to spend so much time discussing perseverance. However, after working with numerous individuals through the years, I have seen first-hand the critical role perseverance plays in one's life, including my own. Perseverance can make one reach levels of success one could've never imagined. Yet a lack of this thing called *'perseverance'* in one's life and it will lead one to receive the opposite of the results they want. Therefore, one should always remind oneself that anything they desire in life is reachable, regardless of their life circumstances or background, as long as they choose to believe in themselves and utilise perseverance.

7

Circumstances mean nothing

One of the most common excuses individuals use to justify anything that goes wrong in their lives or when they are not living the life they seek is 'circumstance.'

- "If I were just born into a rich family, I wouldn't be poor."
- "If I went to a private school and didn't go to a school full of poor kids, things would've been better."
- "Nothing goes right in my life; maybe if I were born in a different town, everything would've been better."
- "If I didn't marry this person, my life could've been so different."
- "If I didn't meet this person, everything would have been great in my life."
- "Why do I have such a crappy job?"

- *"Why do I have no money?"*

These are just a few examples of the many excuses individuals use each day to rationalise why their lives are the way they are. You may be one of those individuals or know of one who constantly blames life circumstances for everything that goes wrong within their lives. Unfortunately, the real disappointment here is not in the circumstances life has bestowed upon them but rather the belief that life circumstances are to blame for how their lives are or have turned out. You see, circumstances do not dictate our achievements and failures in life. Instead, it is you and the thoughts you hold. Throughout this book, we have referenced one's *'physical reality,'* which translates to one's 3D world. This is the world you see, touch, and hear. When things are going wrong in one's physical reality, one blames their environment, upbringing, or others for their shortcomings. This is not the case, and why we encourage all who read this book not to judge their lives based on their past or current physical reality or circumstances but rather learn to focus on good-feeling thoughts.

Regrettably, most individuals associate their thoughts with what they are observing, i.e., circumstance. Seeing something delightful around them makes them feel satisfying, happy thoughts. But, if they see something dreadful, they have awful unpleasant thoughts. This forces individuals to believe they cannot control their feelings because of the circumstances they have just observed. This then influences an individual to go through life trying to control their circumstances. However, no matter how much an individual tries to control circumstances in their physical reality, there will always be some new circumstance that will force the individual back to feeling unpleasant thoughts. Think about your own life. Has everything in your life been perfect and gone your way? I am sure we would all agree that this would most likely not be the case.

When you take the time to be a deliberate creator rather than an observer of your life, you open yourself up to a world that will bring great joy, achievements, and pleasure. Deliberate creation aims to understand how the thoughts and feelings one has can change the circumstances one is living in the physical world, bringing you all that you desire, rather than the other way around. Individuals who are consciously aware of this and their thoughts will have no trouble reflecting this in their physical reality.

Deliberate creation can be broken down into three easy steps:

1. Having good feelings, and positive thoughts about what you desire
2. Expecting to receive that of which you desire, with no thoughts of doubt & self-limiting beliefs
3. Seeing the results of your desire in your physical reality

You should only concern yourself with steps one and two during the deliberate creation process. When one wastes time thinking, *"When will my results come to me?"* all they do is create a vibrational lack in the creative process. This means you will not see the results you seek and will be in severe misalignment with that of which you desire. When this happens, the individual in question will continue to attract and live through the same circumstances they were trying to get rid of in the first instance. Furthermore, it also means that you have not yet fully understood how to rid yourself of negative and self-limiting beliefs.

If this is the case, we strongly suggest you go back and read the previous chapters to comprehend the significance of this concept in detail. Only then can you get into the proper vibrational state of being a deliberate creator of your life and understand that life circumstances are genuinely irrelevant. If an individual gets too caught up in their current or previous life circumstances, they will not be able to move towards a life filled with contentment and joy. You are the master of your life, not your circumstances.

It does not matter what you have experienced, your upbringing, race, or social status; if you have something that you want to achieve, you can. For example, since I was a child, I have always wanted to be a writer and write a children's series. I did not come from a family of writers or a family born in my birth country Australia. I am a child of Turkish Cypriot migrants and went to school with other migrant kids in what was considered a low socio-economic neighbourhood at the time. There are not many Australian Turkish Cypriot writers, yet here I am, following my life purpose. Had I paid attention to my life 'circumstances' or lacked the belief I would succeed, I wouldn't be writing this book. I could've easily said, what does a child from a community who is a minority in the writing world understand about writing books. Yet, I did not let such thoughts consume me; instead, I let my belief system guide me. I entered the writing world in the children's literature space, then shifted my path and began writing articles about everyday life and the concepts in this book, some of which reached the trending list of some sites. I watched as my books and writing went to different countries worldwide and began to receive speaking and media opportunities. In addition to this, I would receive messages from individuals worldwide telling me how my writing inspired them to take action or how much their kids enjoyed my children's series. Circumstances genuinely do not matter. My life circumstances have never stopped me from following my passions, and your life circumstances shouldn't stop you from pursuing your passions either. You are a deliberate creator with the power to achieve whatever you desire, regardless of your life circumstances. As long as you have those positive, good feeling thoughts and the belief system to match, you will be able to reach your destination. You may come across obstacles, yes, but you will never be without the ability to get to where you need to go.

8

Create your own habits & routine

We hear a lot about creating healthy habits and routines in order to thrive. And yes, while routine and good habits assist one in prospering and reaching their goals, it is equally important to create habits and routines that fit within one's OWN lifestyle. Not one individual goes about their day in the same manner. What works for one person may not work for you. Do not try to replicate another person's routine or habit unless it fits perfectly well with your lifestyle, or you will cause yourself to be in a state of distress. When an individual tries to force a new routine or habit upon themselves that does not necessarily match their needs or goals, it will cause vibrational discord between what one hopes to achieve and their physical reality. You will set yourself up to fail when this happens and have low vibrational feelings such as stress, anger, frustration, and sadness. When an individual gets caught up in intense low vibrational feelings, it is much more challenging to adhere to a new routine and habit. Routines and habits are supposed to be simple and easy, not the other way around.

Through my many interactions with individuals and clients, I have discovered that they get overly excited when setting new goals and habits. There is nothing wrong with a bit of excitement and happiness. In fact, we encourage it. However, there is a fine line between excitement and being overly motivated, which can cause an individual to take on more things than they can actually handle. For example, the most common habit individuals try to change is the time they get up. They hear from gurus and experts who say waking up earlier in the mornings is excellent. And yes, while waking up earlier may make some feel like a million dollars, if you are not a morning person, attempting to get up at an exceptionally earlier time than usual will only make you more miserable. Thus, why we put an emphasis on ensuring new habits or routines you create are ones that will suit your lifestyle.

Another critical component of habit and routine creation is starting small. Do not try to overhaul your habits and routine all in one go. Instead, work on making small and incremental changes each day, as it will be much easier for you to adhere to when that is the case.

Living a successful life means an individual feels contentment and fulfilment in all areas of life, including their routine and habits. But one cannot find the contentment and fulfilment they desire if they are making such drastic changes to their lives that it only brings them misery. Throughout this book, time and time, we have mentioned that an individual must be in alignment with what they desire and their physical reality. The same applies to habits and routines. An individual must be in alignment with what it is they seek from their new habits and routine. Always ask yourself: *"What am I seeking with this action?"* If you find yourself unhappy with your reply, it is safe to say you are not yet in vibrational harmony with what you wish to achieve from this new habit or routine and should seek an alternative method.

Another good tip for new habits and routines is to schedule. When one allocates a specific time to adhere to their recent lifestyle change, it is easier for the individual to stick to it. I personally love a good schedule, but that most likely has to do with me being a very routine-oriented individual. Scheduling gives me a feeling of happiness and organisation when it comes to my day. I am in a position where I must be highly considerate of how I spend my hours throughout the day, as I have much to do. For example, some days, I will have to get up at odd morning hours to chat with clients who reside in different countries to mine or take part in overseas interviews for my books. Furthermore, besides writing books, I am also a contributing writer to various publications, so I must make time for that also. Whatever it may be, scheduling is my best friend in my line of work.

Allocating specific times within your schedule will always be an excellent start to adjusting to new habits or routines. For example, if someone wants to lose weight and is exceptionally time-poor, they will find it challenging to assign time to exercise. However, if they were only to schedule five minutes per day to exercise during the week and then gradually increase their activity time by an additional five minutes the following weeks, it would be much easier to incorporate into their lives. And, after some time, their new habit and routine will become second nature to them. Small steps and schedules are the best things an individual can use to establish new routines and habits in their lives.

Changes in one's habits and routine does not have to be over the top. One can even begin by taking time to make their bed each morning or ensuring they have enough time for breakfast. For example, I will never leave the house without making my bed. It seems simple enough, but it has become part of my morning routine. This may seem like a chore to others, but to me, it's just second nature. When a habit or routine becomes second nature to you, that is when you know you have indeed succeeded in creating a healthy pattern when it comes to your new habits and or routine. New habits or routines need not be complicated; they only need to serve your purpose and more significant goals. One could argue, well, how does making your bed fit your purpose? And my answer to that would be that it ensures I start my day organised. I follow particular habits throughout my working day, and regardless of how little or big those habits may be, it all has a purpose in my life and what I do. And this again comes back to lifestyle. When creating habits or routines, no matter how big or small, you must consider that it serves you and your purpose, not anyone else.

As we conclude this chapter, it is worth mentioning that one is never too old or too young to create new habits or routines within their life. Regardless of our status in life, we can all make small changes to live a fulfilling and joyful life.

9

The art of saying 'no'

Has there been a time in your life, or perhaps even in the workplace, where you said yes to something, not because you necessarily agreed with it but rather out of obligation?

One would assume that your answer to that question would be a 'yes,' as it is all too common for individuals to constantly say yes to something they do not necessarily agree with or support. Individuals often do this to either keep the peace and avoid conflict or because they do not want to deal with the tiring energy that would ensue if they were to say no. Even today, the fear of saying 'no' to our spouses, partners, friends, bosses, or work colleagues is all too real. In contrast, while some have mastered the art of learning to say no, most individuals have not, particularly in workplaces.

Through my observations, while working with clients from various industries, I have found that the fear of saying no is more frequent in my female clients than in males. This has to do with how women have been programmed and perceived, especially throughout history, where there was an expectation they would remain silent and not speak their minds. However, it is promising to see that women have now begun to find their voice and speak their truth, as it should be. While there is still much to do in this space, including ridding some women of the cultural programming that has limited their ability to pursue their endeavours, it is beautiful to witness many others come to the forefront through their work successes. I was fortunate enough to grow up in a household and family where it did not matter whether you were male or female. We were able to express our opinions, and as my parents would always say to me, *"You can be whatever you want to be in this world if you put your mind to it,"* and *"Do what you want, not what others want."* It may be why I have never had any issues saying no in the workplace or knocking back lower-paying salaries when offered. Not because I was better than anyone else, but because I knew what I could bring to an organisation and my worth. Knowing one's worth plays an important factor in saying no and can particularly assist one in workplace settings and negotiating salaries or hourly pay rates. While we will go through a few tools to assist you in learning the art of saying 'no,' nothing is of more value than knowing one's worth.

ONE'S WORTH

How you see yourself will always be more important than how others see you, including your family, friends, or superiors in the office. The sense of self-worth a person possesses is a measurement of how much they value themselves. Self-worth is embracing and showing oneself respect, dignity, and understanding. Through the good and the bad, it is the ability to love who you are and everything you will be. We are constantly evolving through this life, learning through various experiences.

Interestingly though, as one matures and ages, one often seems to forget the importance of self-worth and self-kindness. In the early years of our lives, between the ages of 0 and 3, we seldom wonder about our self-worth, nor do we have issues with it. Instead, we grow fascinated with our surroundings, imagination, and the individuals around us. In this phase of our lives, our self-worth is almost limitless, so why do we forget it as we mature?

Think of all the rare jewels in this world. Not one is the same. As each shines differently and comes made of a different cut, each becomes moulded into a different shape without losing its value. The same principles apply to you. You were born as a rare jewel. No one else is you in this world, so why would you dim your shine by undervaluing yourself?

When individuals value and understand their self-worth, they don't settle for less or permit themselves to flounder in others' mediocracy. Instead, they shine just like they were supposed to when first placed on this planet. But, more importantly, they also learn to say no to things that don't serve their greater purpose, whether in a job or in life.

Individuals who know their worth are typically more adept at saying no. But, every individual should be able to say no rather than agree to things that don't necessarily support their greater purpose or goals.

The simple four-step guide below is here to assist you in learning the ability to say 'no' effectively, whether in work or other areas of your life:

1. Personal interest

A lot of individuals fear that when they put themselves first or their needs over others, they are essentially being selfish. This is particularly common when an individual wants to say no, but instead sits and agrees to whatever is proposed by another party, be that a friend, work colleague, or boss. While the person struggles with saying no, they fail to see that whatever the situation, or whoever is asking them for something, is also being selfish and thinking of their own 'personal interests.' While this is not a bad thing, it should serve as a friendly reminder that you should also look out for your own personal interests. Of course, let this not be construed. Individuals who ask something of you are not necessarily selfish in a negative way. We simply state that when one asks for something from someone, they also have an invested interest in the outcome or situation.

For example, let us say your employer has asked you to do something outside your position description or to take on a higher role with the same pay. In this situation, we can see that the other party has an invested interest in getting you to do more work for less money. If you think this is an excellent stepping stone to getting a work promotion, that's fine. However, if you are one who realises that agreeing to such a thing would only lower your overall worth, you would also be most accurate in your observation. When faced with a situation where one feels a strong obligation to say yes but would rather say no, one should always ask themselves, *"What will I gain from this situation if I was to say yes?"* or *"How does what they're asking me to do, impact me and my needs?"*

If you find that both answers are negative and do not serve or suit your personal interest, you should say no. One should never fear saying no or doing what's right for them.

Now, let us suppose the same employer offers you a work promotion but this time with a higher paying salary. However, you have a side-hustle, and your long-term goal has always been to work for yourself and leave your current role when possible. While a promotion may seem like a great opportunity from the employer's perspective, it will prevent you from having the extra time to concentrate on your long-term goal. So, again, one would need to consider their personal interest and needs rather than acting out of obligation and saying yes because it is an excellent opportunity from an employer. Anytime one says yes to something one does not necessarily agree with, one essentially says no to oneself and their life purpose. Remember this statement when you struggle to stay true to yourself and your needs.

2. Satisfaction

Could you imagine what a world we'd live in if everyone loved what they did or followed their life purpose? For starters, the early morning commute to town would not be filled with such unhappy-looking individuals, that's for sure. Think about it, when a person gets up in the morning to go to a job or appointment they hate, they will always wake with a feeling of misery and other low vibrational feelings. People can never find the satisfaction they seek when doing the things they do not enjoy or have agreed to out of obligation. When one completes any task for an extended period they are not satisfied with, they will suffer from burnout and other similar issues that will impact their mental health and wellbeing in a negative way. This is all the more reason to learn to say no to what others ask of you when it does not bring you any sort of satisfaction.

Satisfaction in all areas of our lives is what leads to a prosperous and harmonious-filled life and will always bring you from a state of misery to a state of happiness. On the other hand, if you continually choose to do things that do not satisfy your inner being, you will always live a life filled with disappointment. Additionally, constantly trying to agree to everyone's needs, views, or wants is extremely tiring and will never bring satisfaction to us.

3. Speak with confidence

If one can show confidence, belief, and emotion when speaking, one's response will be better received and will relinquish the opportunity for push-back in most situations. It is an excellent skill to acquire if you are lacking in this area.

You should always maintain an even tone when speaking and try not to finish any statements they make with an open-ended question. The idea is to take control of the situation rather than the other way around. When one gives power to the other party, it is extremely hard for an individual to hold their ground when saying no. An excellent way to remind oneself to speak confidently is to think of previous speakers you have come across at seminars or webinars. Which speaker got your attention, the one who bore you to death or the one who spoke with confidence and emotion?

An individual who speaks with confidence will always be well received. Moreover, speaking with confidence is critical if you want to decline an offer articulately, do not forget this.

4. Don't compare yourself

When one surrounds themselves with individuals or team members who constantly say yes to everything, it is easy for them to fall into the trap of feeling obligated to say yes as well. Fortunately, it need not be that way. One should always see themselves as an individual entity and understand that what may suit one's friends or work colleagues may not suit them, including saying yes to everything. All individuals have different needs and lead different lives. Not one person is the same. This even extends to workplaces where each individual goes about completing their work tasks in a different style and manner. For example, if your fellow work colleagues get excited about doing an additional ten tasks on top of their current workload, good for them, but know that you do not have to operate in the same manner. There is nothing wrong with being or doing things differently! One does not have to say yes to something because everyone else has or "it's the right thing to do." There is nothing righteous about doing something an individual disagrees with, and you are always entitled to decline an offer or suggestion that does not sit well with you. Never compare yourself to those around you or try to replicate their behaviour if it is not who or what you want to be. You have the right to do what you want and feel is appropriate to you and no one else.

At first, when you begin exercising the above tips in your daily life, you may feel out of your comfort zone, but rest assured, after a few times, it will become second nature to you. It is your divine right to decline all that does not serve or bring you fulfilment in this life. It would help if you always remind yourself of this, particularly in workplace settings. It does not matter where you sit on the corporate ladder or work. You do not have to oblige to the demands placed on yourself by others. The only person one is obligated to serve is oneself.

10

Find your balance

I recently attended a seminar and course run by a well-known PR guru where they proudly announced, *"There is no such thing as work-life balance if you want to succeed."* As an individual who not only takes work-life balance seriously and encourages it, one can imagine the look of horror that appeared on my face after hearing such a statement. At that moment, I also wondered about the new graduates taking part in the seminar and the unsafe messaging they were receiving. Living a life filled with success is not one where you work yourself into the grave and is not the messaging we should be promoting. If it's one thing I've learned about success and living a fulfilled life, it's that it goes hand in hand with a healthy work-life balance. Even if an individual is currently unemployed, one still needs to find a healthy balance between their daily tasks and the amount of time they dedicate to doing whatever it is they love.

The era of working hard to succeed is long gone. We are now in an age where it is encouraged to work smarter, not harder. Hard work alone will not bring you the riches you desire from life. Being genuinely rich in life means being rich in all areas, not just through one's bank account. One does not have to sacrifice their family life or the time one spends with their children to get to where one needs to be. If an individual doesn't get the formula of balance right, they will suffer from burnout, anxiety, and other illnesses, resulting in being in a negative mental space. Unfortunately, this is not something that will only impact them. It will also affect the relationships a person holds dear to themselves also.

> "FINDING BALANCE IN ONE'S LIFE IS LIKE FINDING THE RIGHT MUSICAL NOTES TO CREATE A BEAUTIFUL HARMONIOUS MELODY."

When there is no balance, the musical notes of your life will not be in harmony but rather in disarray. Conversely, leading a balanced life means all areas of one's life should work together to create a magical and abundant-filled life.

Often when striving to find balance in our lives, individuals try to do more than they can actually manage. They create extra-long to-do lists and then try to get through all the tasks they've jotted down within a day. The issue is not with the tasks themselves but the emphasis on completing them as quickly as possible throughout the day. If the individual fails to meet their deadline, they begin to associate with negative low vibrational feelings. On the other hand, if they complete their tasks, it often comes with a sense of exhaustion, not the good high-flying vibrations one would expect from an individual who has balance in their lives. Balance is not about the number of tasks you can complete during the day. It is about ensuring all areas of your life work and blend well together!

The best step an individual can take towards living a balanced life is to learn how to switch on and off. This means learning how to set boundaries and limits on your work times and being able to switch off when that allocated time comes around. This technique applies to those working and those who may be stay-at-home parents or unemployed. Whatever you do, you should never trade your 'personal' time or sleep for work or house chores. Of course, there will be those of us who love to work overtime, and if that brings you joy, go for it. As long as you are happy and content with your life, that is all that matters. However, for the large number of individuals who would prefer not to be overworked and exhausted, learning to switch on and off is crucial. No good ever comes from overworking or using your 'personal' time at home to think about work-related issues when you want a healthy balanced lifestyle.

Other elements crucial to having balance in one's life are prioritisation and time management. Therefore, it is encouraged you allocate approximately 1 hour to 30 minutes per day or a few hours on the weekend to yourself. This time is only to relax, unwind and do activities that align you with your higher self. Such an activity that is ideally suited for this purpose is meditation. Meditation can help reduce stress and promote calmness and clarity in one's body. It can be done for as long or as short as you like and can fit within anyone's lifestyle.

To meditate:

1. Find a quiet spot
2. Sit in a comfortable position
3. Breath gently
4. Allow distractions to flow in and out *(It is common for your mind to wander during meditation, particularly if it is not something you are accustomed to. Acknowledge any good or bad thought that comes to you, but do not think much of it. Instead, bring your focus back to your breathing.)*

While meditation is a great practice, you can also do other activities to help you relax and unwind. For example, if you are an individual who loves the outdoors, then make time to sit in nature and take in the fresh air while listening to the beautiful sounds you are surrounded by. You can also choose to sit in a quiet spot and journal about all the beautiful things or individuals you are grateful for. Whatever task one decides to complete for this activity, it would be wise to avoid using technological gadgets to connect with oneself wholly.

Connecting to one's higher self is of utmost importance when creating balance in one's life. It ensures you have a deeper understanding of yourself and your inner being while assisting you in taking better care of your body. An individual should always take time to pamper themselves and look after the one thing they carry around with them each day – one's body. This can be anything from getting a massage once a week or once a month to allocating 5 minutes a day to a new skincare routine or spending some time working out. Whatever it may be, always make time to look after your body.

Your body is the most important thing you have to look after. It is the one thing that stays with us till the end of time, so we have a duty of care to protect it. But, just as we try to care for our bodies, we also need to look after our most prized possession, the mind.

When trying to juggle a healthy balanced life, one often forgets to take care of and protect their mind from any of the negative influences they have around them. Instead, they enable others or situations to change their moods and take away from their positive mindset. To have inner peace and happiness, one must try to stay away from or limit any interactions with individuals who are toxic in nature. This can be hard at times but needed if you want to upgrade your life to one of fulfilment.

One would agree to have balance in one's life; one must utilise all areas of their life. The trick is not to get overwhelmed with finding balance in your life, but rather to look at how you can incorporate the above techniques to create synchrony and balance in your life. Just as a jigsaw puzzle comes together piece by piece, your life can come together, but only if you take the time to learn how to organise your life's pieces harmoniously. When this happens, one will always be bound to create a life filled with success and one of balance.

11

Let relationships be easy

    There is nothing more complex in this world than the relationships one has with the individuals they are surrounded by or the ones who come and go in their lives. We are not only talking about romantic relationships, but every human interaction you have and will have in this life, from friends to family to your relationship with your work colleagues or teachers. Each relationship leaves some sort of lasting impression in one's mind, whether positive or negative. Think back to a time when you met someone and had an immediate dislike towards them or another time when you met someone and had an instantaneous connection to the individual or individuals in question. There are also times when two parties can come across each other, and for reasons unknown to one another, without even uttering a word, a mutual dislike between the parties will occur or vice versa. Human interactions are indeed a strange phenomenon, but they do not have to be complicated.

All relationships should be healthy and enable the opportunity for growth and respectful dialogue between the parties. However, there will be times when one will come across individuals who simply choose not to see and respect their views, opinions, or boundaries. This is even more evident in workplace settings where one has a condescending and egocentric boss. These two unflattering traits seem to be more common in leaders who lack the skill and experience to do their job. Therefore, they try to compensate for their lack of skills by trying to bring others down, often the ones who have to report to them. Whenever one comes across an individual, who does not respect their boundaries or views, even if it is your boss, one should move on or, where relevant, seek assistance from another party to help resolve the issue. No one needs to feel like their opinions or views do not matter. Any thought one has, good or bad, is always valid.

Healthy relationships require effective communication, which means having the ability to express your opinions and the ability to listen. All effective partnerships, be it romantic or friendship, are based on mutual respect where one can freely express their feelings and opinions and meet the other's core needs. This also applies to those in business partnerships or individuals who share a similar purpose in life.

When one aligns with an individual or group of people with similar goals, they find it easier to work towards attaining their goals and definite purpose in life. This is because the relationship is harmonious and provides a platform to motivate and inspire one another to greatness. It is a place to acquire knowledge from each other and to grow one's mind to that of a success mindset. Individuals who spend more time with goal-oriented and passionate people are always more likely to succeed in their endeavours than those who continually associate with negative individuals who have a terrible attitude. Success and fulfilment depend on an individual's mindset. By associating or forming relationships with individuals who carry or display the characteristics one seeks, one will always find the path to success easier to reach.

Of course, there is no such thing as a perfect relationship, but there is such a thing as having mutual understanding between parties. Anytime there is discord in a relationship, it will fail. One must be in harmony with the individuals they choose to let into their lives if one is to feel content and fulfilment in their lives. This applies to every human interaction one has in their lifetime. All relationships need to be pleasant in nature, which is why one should always take a conscious approach to who or what one permits into their life. Yet, one should also be mindful when it comes to honesty and criticism in a relationship, as there is a very fine line between the two. When one is honest in a relationship and expresses their feelings, the other should still feel respected and valued. The one who provides honest feedback to the other should deliver whatever it is they want to say constructively and not in a hurtful manner. If one considers being 'honest' the opportunity to criticise or belittle the other person, then that is not a healthy and mature relationship.

While one expects maturity to be the norm in one's relationship, it is not a concept every individual can display or understand. For example, I once worked with a boss who would choose to argue with any individual who would express an alternative view, followed by giving them the silent treatment. One would wonder how such an arrogant and rude individual would be in a leadership position, let alone on such a high-paying salary, but there they were. Their immature behaviour did not benefit anyone and impacted the productivity levels of the entire team, so much so that there was also an extremely high staff turnover rate. I was a university graduate at the time and there, luckily for a short period, but I could never quite fathom why a middle-aged individual would behave in such a child-like manner. You may have an individual in your life who displays similar characteristics. If this is the case, it would be rather hard for the individual in question to respect or consider any of your views. These individuals do not have the capacity or display the level of maturity you do. Therefore, limiting your interactions with such toxic individuals would be wise or, even better, ridding yourself of such an unhealthy relationship altogether. You should never engage with individuals who do not bring positive-high vibrational feelings to yourselves.

Sometimes, we can also outgrow individuals who no longer align with our lifestyle or thoughts. Whatever the reason, it is also okay to let go of those individuals you once considered yourself closest to. One must always take the time to focus on one's life and embrace their growth and the person they are becoming. It would be safe to say that when you reflect on your life, you would realise that the thoughts that you now have are most likely not the same thoughts you had when you were younger.

We are continually growing in wisdom, and with each new age one enters, we learn more and more about ourselves.

Of course, each individual will grow at different rates. An individual who chooses to remain stuck doing the same thing over and over will not grow at the same rate as one who creates opportunities for themselves. When two or more parties begin travelling on different paths, it is often the time when individuals start to separate or grow apart from one another. This is because each of us travels at a different speed. This is not to say that their paths will not align again in the future. It only means these two or more parties have chosen to evolve differently.

For example, when I secured my first proper job as a university graduate, I became friends with the other graduate girls in my workplace. It was a lovely friendship, but as time passed, my goals in life changed, and I did not want to rot away at some job I didn't even enjoy. But, on the other hand, my new graduate friends at the time were perfectly content in carrying on the same way in their lives and doing the same job. So, where I chose to pursue my goals and develop my skills and self, they decided to stay in the same organisation and role. Years after I had left this particular organisation and advanced myself in my field of expertise at the time, I got offered a position at the same organisation I had started in all those many years ago. Of course, this position was much higher than where I had begun those many years ago as a graduate. Upon my return to this organisation, I was surprised to see the same individuals I once worked side by side with and had a friendship with, in the same role, getting paid the same salary. I pondered why anyone would permit themselves to stay stagnant and limit themselves when so many other opportunities were available if they had only chosen to invest in themselves. The same individuals then came up and congratulated me on how well I'd done for myself, all while telling me how they were sick of working in the same boring role they had since graduating from university. I didn't say much, but I could see that I had done the right thing by separating myself from those who chose not to develop themselves. And this is the thing about our relationships with individuals, while we may share a journey at some time of our lives with one another, we can also grow and drift apart. And that is perfectly okay.

Part of living a successful and abundant life is by having harmonious relationships with one another. Relationships only become difficult when we permit them to be difficult. Where you can, be selective of the individuals you align with and do not settle for any relationships that do not align with your life path or bring you joy. Relationships with one another should be easy and enjoyable, not the other way round. Sure, there will be times when we may separate our lives from one another, but if someone is supposed to be in your life, your paths will indeed align once again.

12

Let go of fear

Fear is a common human emotion experienced by every individual at one time or another in their lives. It usually stems from when there is a real threat of harm to ourselves but can also arise through the imagination, through the perceptions we hold in our minds. There is not one person in the world who is immune to the emotion of fear. It is an emotion of such significant influence that it can stop even the brightest individuals from living their best lives and experiencing the success they seek.

It comes in various forms and impacts each of us differently. Some may go through life fearing poverty, while another can go through life fearing bad health or even the loss of those they love. There is no one-size-fits-all when it comes to dealing with fear; however, we can do our best to try and learn different techniques and tailor them to our specific situation to assist us in overcoming our fears.

Every one of us will have to deal with fear at some point, but we must also recognise fear for what it is: a powerful source for growth and success.

We have grown so accustomed to seeing fear in a negative light that we have failed to see the many benefits that fear gifts us. This may sound peculiar to an individual who is not that familiar with the power of the mind, but it is our hope that reading this book thus far, you have at least begun to come to a deeper understanding of the vibrational being you are and the many benefits this brings to oneself.

I remember as a child, up until the age of five, I had an extreme fear of swimming. My parents would take me to swimming lessons, where I would scream my lungs out to the extent that even swimming instructors would not know what to do with me. I am sure one would agree that water safety is an important thing to learn both for children and adults alike. Although my mother was not the most excellent swimmer, she took it upon herself and my father to take me to the pools every weekend. Slowly but surely, step by step, through their encouragement, I eventually managed to get into the water with no tears or screaming, for that matter. While it was a slow process to get me used to the water, within a short period, I not only became accustomed to the water, but I also went on to become a professional swimmer in my youth. It is rather strange how a child who was so petrified of the water would find a water sport as one of her passions growing up. When I won my first school championship, my teacher, who had known me since prep, even mentioned my extreme fear in his congratulatory speech while handing me my trophy.

When one learns to overcome their fears, new paths begin to show themselves to us. These paths are ones we would have never considered crossing once upon a time had we not taken steps to overcome the fears that hold us back. For example, had I not overcome my fear of water, I would not have become a professional swimmer, nor would I have been able to learn that fear is only as big as we may make it in our minds.

Fear as we know it affects everybody and all sexes. Yet, society has played a pivotal role in teaching us that men should not have any fears or concerns. They have taught individuals to think of men as fearless, brave creatures who are strong and can deal with anything life throws at them. This programming has led to many men being unable to express their emotions adequately or suffering in silence when dealing with issues that cause them anxiety and frustration. The bottling up of their feelings for an extended period and society's expectations have led to many men having intensified feelings of anxiety, suicide, and other negative emotions. We should not set up discriminatory expectations of how the various sexes deal with fear or, in this case, burden them with the expectations of having no fear, as no sex is immune to fear.

For an individual to overcome their fear, one must first correctly identify and learn what is causing them to feel the way they do. Fears live in our subconscious minds and only intensify with time when we do not address them. By taking an in-depth look at the fear one has, one will better understand it in a way they could not have previously. An excellent way to do this is to journal your feelings and the physiological sensations you have when thinking about your fear over a few weeks. Writing down our feelings and sensations associated with our fears helps us to minimise their importance and identify one's individual triggers. When one has a better understanding of their triggers and their association with one's fear, it aids the individual in overcoming these fears more easily.

Another approach to dealing with fear is to not think of fear in the traditional sense but instead, look at fear purely as an avenue to rob ourselves of positive opportunities and experiences. This approach may sound illogical to some, but it enables the feelings of fear to act as a reminder of the things we can lose rather than focusing on the things we are most afraid of. In their right mind, not one individual would knowingly want to rob themselves of the path to success, fulfilment, or riches. By using fear as one's personal reminder, the individual begins to let go and not hold onto the negative emotions associated with their fear as they once did. Over time, by continually using this approach, the individual will find it much easier to align back to their purpose and what they wish to achieve in their lives while letting go of the things that once held them back.

While fear is inevitable in life, it doesn't mean we should let it control our lives or the things we do. When we take on new paths or try new things, we often associate it with the emotions of fear. Nothing scares an individual more than the unknown. When something is unknown to an individual, it makes it easier for them to speculate and come up with different scenarios in one's mind. These scenarios, more often than not, are negative in nature. When you find yourself coming up with the worst possible scenarios in your mind, take a few minutes out of your day, close your eyes, and envision yourself in the complete opposite scenario of the one you had earlier imagined. Take as many minutes as you need, and absorb yourself in the moment and the positive emotions this new scenario is bringing you. Repeat this exercise each day for as long as you need to assist yourself in learning to let go of the fears you harbour.

Most of our fears are unwarranted and not as big as we make them out to be. The best way to make fear a positive part of one's life is by taking action and changing one's perception of fear. The moment you begin to shift your perception is the moment your path to fulfilment and success begins to take shape. Learn this essential step and exercise the above techniques to conquer your life and fears.

13

Procrastination is a vibe killer

Procrastination is a poisonous symptom that impacts nearly every individual in the world. A common yet unhealthy habit, over time, procrastination kills one's ambition and drive for success. Not only that, but it also causes one to avoid matters or essential tasks that need to be addressed or completed. Simply put, procrastination is a vibe killer.

So why do we do it?

Well, for one, humans like instantaneous gratification more than delayed gratification. When someone puts off doing something, often it is because there isn't any immediate reward or gratification available to the individual if they were to complete the task or have a difficult conversation. For example, let us say you are a student at university and the deadline for your assignment is looming. The assignment will form part of your overall grade for the semester. You have had the assignment for weeks, but instead of getting a start on it, you choose to spend your time going out with friends or watching TV.

Now let us change the scenario and say you have the same assignment to complete but with some new conditions this time. With the new arrangement, you could graduate immediately if you completed the assignment and turned it in, thus avoiding spending the standard duration it would have otherwise taken you to get your degree. It would be safe to assume that any individual with such an offer would rush off and complete their assignment without giving it a second thought. This is because upon completing this task, one would be rewarded and receive instantaneous gratification knowing they would no longer have to waste any more time at school to obtain their degree. In comparison, in the other scenario, there would be a delay in the person receiving any benefit or gratification for completing their assignment, making it easier to procrastinate.

No one wants to wait to see the fruits of their labour flourish. Instead, many individuals have a desire for instantaneous results. And this is where the issue of procrastination lies. Procrastination exists because individuals carry a deep desire for immediate gratification. Therefore, the best thing an individual can do to overcome procrastination is to make small changes to how they complete their tasks, ensuring that whatever they do brings them the instant gratification they desperately seek. For example, you could even reward yourself for completing your tasks by giving yourself a small gift. I often gift myself something of significance once a year when I have achieved my yearly goal.

Another method to assist you with procrastination is to have a set routine for completing tasks you do not like to do by allocating specific times to get certain tasks done. It would help if you were particular about the tasks you pick and how you do them. For example, suppose a task is somewhat related to another task. In which case, you should always categorise and complete them on the same day or ensure those similar tasks are conducted simultaneously on specific days. Now, let us pick an easy and popular household task that impacts most individuals and one that most dislike, such as picking clothes off the washing line. One would suppose that after picking up the clothes, one would eventually have to fold the clothes they have gathered, *yes?* And one would also agree that folding clothes isn't that exciting either, *yes?* So here is an example where there isn't much gratification available to the individual, yet it is a task that one must complete. Many individuals dump their clothes in a spare room after picking them up and often let them sit there for a few hours or days. They know they will have to fold their clothes eventually, but instead, they go off and do other things because folding clothes is not appealing. This is procrastination at its finest.

You would remember we spoke about instantaneous gratification and allocating specific times to complete tasks or grouping similar tasks together that we do not enjoy or delay doing, *yes?* Now, if you were to apply these principles to the example provided, as you pick each piece of clothing off the line, you would also fold it right then and there.

Simple enough, yes?

We want to demonstrate how a minor tweak in one's routine

or processes can eliminate a task one would have otherwise delayed or felt discomfort in doing. Overcoming procrastination does not have to be a tricky thing. When individuals implement specific changes to their routine or processes, they can create new habits that begin to rid themselves of negative thinking, including procrastination. This is even more powerful when one combines this with the feelings of instantaneous gratification or a reward for completing their task. The reward itself is of little importance and can be as big or small, and it can even simply be that an individual has more free time to do whatever it is they please. Whatever reward you choose, all that matters is that you can associate what you are doing with feelings of gratification.

Contrary to common belief, the benefit of ridding oneself of procrastination is not only applicable to getting tasks done. Ridding oneself of procrastination also assists one in improving their mental health and well-being while enabling ourselves to excel towards our goals and life purpose. If you know anyone who suffers from continual procrastination, you would have observed them constantly being exhausted and stressed. This is a common symptom of a person who continually chooses to procrastinate. But thankfully, by making some minor tweaks to our lifestyles, we can learn to let go of procrastination. No habit, good or bad, cannot be unlearned, including procrastination.

Through my interactions with clients and friends, I have found that those who lack ambition and drive are also the ones who suffer most from procrastination. In addition, those who lack routine in their lives are also more susceptible to procrastination. Therefore, if one truly desires to live the life they dream of, one cannot permit procrastination into their lives. It may be a hard truth, but one must learn to let go of unhealthy habits when one wants to succeed.

I have been a routine-oriented individual from a young age, so I have never had much time for procrastination. Anytime I had something to do, I would complete it without giving it much thought while ensuring I stayed focused on my bigger goals in life. Through my interactions with clients and friends, I have seen how exercising routine and small changes in habits can assist one in letting go of procrastination. If you are a parent of a young child, I would strongly suggest you teach them about routine and goal setting. When one establishes healthy habits in a child from a young age, they are less likely to deal with procrastination when in adulthood.

My parents were in no way strict, but they instilled in me the importance of routine and goal setting from a young age. This provided me with many benefits in my adulthood, not to mention a strong belief in my ability to get things done. As a child, upon returning from school, I would be fed and then permitted to watch cartoons for a duration of time before doing my homework. This was my routine during weekdays, and on the weekends, if I had homework, this would also need to be completed before I could go off and enjoy my weekend. As I got a little older, I would be up even earlier in the mornings for swimming training before attending school. When returning home from school, I would eat and do my homework before going back to swimming training in the evening. While some may find my childhood routine extreme, it was nothing of such. One cannot put a price on the value of learning routine and healthy habits from a young age, even if one only realises this in adulthood.

These learnings have allowed me to overcome procrastination and get things done, even in times of difficulties or challenges. Sure, procrastination impacts a large percentage of individuals in the world, but you do not have to be in that percentage if you learn to exercise what we have discussed in this chapter.

14

Be willing to be imperfect

Each day we are inundated with images through tv, magazines, and social media of what some individuals perceive to be the *'perfect'* life or the *'perfect'* person. They absorb these images and think if I act, look or be like that, I'll be perfect. When in reality, there is no such thing as being perfect.

"PERFECTIONISM CAN NEVER EXIST."

One should never confuse striving for success as a means of reaching perfectionism. As we have mentioned many times before, success is being abundant in all areas of life. It is being your authentic self and living the life you dream of, not someone else's. Being your authentic self is having the ability and willingness to be imperfect. It is about embracing all that makes you, you. That includes your flaws and fears.

In this book so far, we have taught you tools that will assist you in living the life you dream of and one of fulfilment, not how to achieve perfectionism. Perfectionism is a mere illusion, for no one is perfect in this world. The world is made up of many imperfect individuals, some of whom we will admire and some of whom we will dislike.

We have always encouraged interactions with those one admires and aspires to be like as a way of learning. But, learning from someone you admire is different from seeing that same individual as 'perfect,' for we can assure you that no one goes through life without making any mistakes. Like most things in life, mistakes are inevitable, yet those who seek perfectionism choose to define themselves by the number of mistakes they make or can avoid. This is because they believe that one must be error-free to be content and fulfilled in life.

Perfectionists also choose to value themselves by their accomplishments. If an individual were to come along and strip them of all their achievements or fancy titles, leaving them with no notable achievements in their mind, they would not give much value to themselves. One can never be happy, content, or fulfilled when self-critical of themselves and their accomplishments or lack thereof. Perfectionists, in their pursuit of perfectionism, often form unhealthy attitudes and belief systems and constantly look for ways to improve themselves. While we encourage individuals to learn, grow, and improve themselves, when one does this as a means of achieving perfectionism, one is going about this in the wrong manner and has also not grasped the actual concept of what improving or expanding in life means. Unfortunately, when this is the case, the individual will never truly experience a life that is harmonious and joyous in nature.

It is time individuals stop chasing the idea of perfectionism and embrace their true authentic selves. The first way to do this is to stop selling the perception of being perfect and show the world what you actually have to offer. By offer, we do not mean your skillset; we mean what makes 'you' - who you are and what you want to be.

Ask yourself the following questions:

- *Who am I?*
- *What am I?*
- *What do I love about myself the most?*

As you identify what you love about yourself, you may also recognise what you don't like or find particularly appealing about yourself. This can be anything ranging from your past actions to parts of your physical appearance. However, no matter what it is, you should understand that to accept and live as your true authentic self, your past life experiences and imperfections must be acknowledged and not used as a means to judge yourselves or predict future behaviours.

"IMPERFECTIONS ARE WHAT MAKE US WHO WE ARE."

When an individual begins to recognise this and starts to

live from their authentic self, they connect to their life purpose wholeheartedly; things that used to make them upset, angry, or sad no longer burden the individual as they once did. Part of this is because the individual has recognised and created a proper balance between their inner self (true self) and their physical world. When individuals connect their true selves to their physical world, magic occurs. Things that once seemed unreachable suddenly become attainable as the individual is no longer operating merely in the physical world but also at a deeper vibrational level. The moment one begins to do this, a sense of calmness and peace arises in the individual's body as they grow to accept and embrace their imperfections while starting to understand their authentic core values. When this happens, you are no longer taking action based on others' needs or wants but instead taking action based on your own core values.

Each individual's core values differ from one another and are dependent on a person's own life experiences. For example, while most individuals choose honesty as a core value, others may prefer deceitfulness over honesty. Of course, it is our hope that your values do not align with things that can bring harm or pain to others, but it is important to note that an individual's values will change throughout their lives as they go through various personal or career changes.

To assist you in identifying your current core values, we have created a brief list of values for you. We would recommend you go down the list and write down the ones that most resonate with you:

- Abundance
- Accomplishments
- Affection
- Ambition
- Appreciation
- Balance
- Caring
- Compassion
- Connection
- Diversity
- Equality
- Fairness
- Faith
- Family
- Forgiveness
- Freedom
- Grace
- Gratitude
- Growth
- Happiness
- Harmony
- Health
- Honesty
- Humanity
- Innovation
- Integrity
- Intuition
- Joy
- Kindness

- Knowledge
- Leadership
- Love
- Loyalty
- Optimism
- Passion
- Patience
- Prosperity
- Relationships
- Religion
- Resilience
- Respect
- Security
- Spirituality
- Stability
- Success
- Teamwork
- Wellness
- Wisdom

Knowing how to identify one's core values will make it much easier for people to determine whether their daily decisions align with their true authentic selves when taking on a new job or setting a new goal. On the other hand, a person may drift further and further away from their core values and authentic selves if the tasks they take on cause them to be at odds with their quest for success or ability to fit in with their surroundings. Therefore, it is of great importance for a person to stay true to their inner core values and authentic selves if they want to receive the success and fulfilment they desire in their lives. You are not here to conform to the ways of the world or others; you are here to be you and do the things that make your true authentic self shine. You are not here to be the 'who' others *"think you should be,"*

Embrace your flaws, imperfections, blemishes, and everything that makes you who you are, and share *YOUR* magic with the world!

15

Be your own agent

I remember when I first started my writing journey, no one knew who I was. All I had was a vision and the belief to succeed. I started in the children's literature space with a dream of sharing my children's series with the world. I wanted my books to teach children to embrace each other as is, regardless of how one may look, act or sound. I could not have predicted how my writing journey would evolve, but I did know where I wanted to go. So, armed with nothing else but my vision and purpose, I became my own PR agent..*literally!*

I didn't have any media contacts at the time but made it my business to get in front of the right people. I pitched and promoted myself and my book series to various publications and managed to get myself invited onto multiple radio stations to promote my new books. As the old saying goes, *"Where there's a will, there's a way."*

If you want to succeed, you need to be your biggest cheerleader. No one will give credit to you or what you say, let alone invest in you, if you do not believe in what you have to offer or your ideas. The most important investment one can make is in themselves.

Unfortunately, individuals fail to see that at the end of the day, we are all our own publicists, whether we intend to be or not. Even when you enter a job interview, you become a publicist, trying to impress and sell yourself to the hiring executives, but it doesn't end there. Think about the time you first met your partner's parents or family. Again, chances are, you would most likely have been acting in the capacity of a publicist again. We could go on and on, as the lists are endless, but the bottom line is this – we are all walking PR agencies at one time or another.

My writing journey didn't progress to where it is now by pure luck. It happened because I believed in myself, what I had to offer, and my definite purpose in life. I didn't doubt that children would enjoy my books, nor did I believe people would dislike what I had to offer. I focused on my end goal, becoming a writer and sharing my work with the world. If I didn't become my own PR agent, I would not have been able to be invited by different publications to share my work and books with everyone, nor would my journey have led me to write this very book you are currently reading.

There may be some of you who may not feel confident about acting as your PR agent or sharing your work and skills with the world. And while you could hire a professional PR company and pay for their services, including marketing and advertising, no one knows better than what you have to offer.

"THE KEY TO YOUR SUCCESS IS NOT DEPENDENT ON WHAT OTHERS DO; RATHER, WHAT YOU CAN DO FOR YOURSELF DETERMINES YOUR SUCCESS."

In order to succeed, one must develop the strength and confidence in themselves to accomplish whatever it is they desire, and that can only start with oneself. You are your beginning and your end. You can either be your biggest fan or choose to be your worst enemy. The choice is yours.

Sure, there will be those who critique one's work or even dislike what one may do or offer, but they will always be a minority compared to those who will love what you do and your work. You are here to shine, not sit in a glass cabinet collecting dust.

For those that may feel they lack the confidence or belief to be their own PR agent, you can try the below exercise to help you:

- *Take a piece of paper*
- *Divide the paper into three separate sections*
- *List three things you are good at in the first section*
- *List three challenges you have overcome in life in the second section*
- *List three achievements or personal qualities that you are most proud of in the third section*
- *Read or update this list once a month or fortnightly*

Some individuals may need a little hand to realise how wonderful and brilliant they truly are. But by regularly setting up small reminders of one's achievements and positive qualities, one may begin to familiarise themselves with a new way of thinking. This will enable the individual to increase their confidence and give them the boost they need to feel more comfortable promoting themselves and their work when required.

There are a lot of individuals who want to stand out from the crowd, but only a select few actually achieve this; *why?*

Because only a few dare to put themselves out there and promote themselves and their work. Some individuals may even have people around them who say, *"Don't do that, you will embarrass yourself,"* or *"Don't be silly, no one is going to be interested in your idea,"* Do not let the nay-sayers interfere with your potential to attain success and live the life you seek. The individuals who tell you you're crazy for trying to put yourself out there are the same ones who will continue to live mediocre lives. Everyone has the right to choose how they want to live, but if you have picked up this book, there is a good chance that you no longer wish to live an average life. You want to succeed and live the life you deserve and desire. *And so you should!*

No one can stop you once you have gained the confidence and willpower to promote yourself and your services. But to become the best PR agent for yourself, one must also have an in-depth understanding of their target audience to promote their services and ideas effectively. So, ask yourself, *"Who are the people that would most benefit from my services or ideas?"*

You would be surprised how many individuals choose to skip this vital step or do not even take the time to conduct thorough research on their target audience. For example, you would expect that if you have an idea or service that would most benefit the education sector, you would not go out and try to network with someone from the food or entertainment industry. Yet, as silly as this may sound, it is common for individuals to attempt to network with people from industries who have no benefit to what they are trying to offer or sell, all because they want to try and "get themselves out there."

While we encourage you to network to promote yourself and your services, you must also be selective with those you choose to interact with while networking. You do not want to spend time promoting yourselves or your services to an individual or organisation with no genuine interest in what it is you are offering. When one has an in-depth understanding of their target audience, it is much easier to get in front of the right people instead of those who do not care about what it is you do.

When you have worked to establish who your target audience is, it would also be of benefit to ask yourself the following questions:

- *What sort of publications does my target audience read?*
- *Which journalists or media outlets cover stories that relate to my niche market?*

The answer to the second question will be of most significance to you, so do not skip it. If you want to be an effective and efficient PR agent for yourself, you need to learn about which people can be of assistance to you in spreading your message wide and far.

Some believe that contacting every well-known journalist or media outlet is the most effective and efficient way to spread the word about their services or share their stories with the world. However, this is one of the biggest mistakes you can make. Being your biggest fan and promoting your story and services isn't about getting in front of as many people as possible. It is about getting in front of the RIGHT people. Do not forget this when you begin to promote yourself and what you do. Nor should one forget that someone will always be interested in what we have to say or offer.

We all have a voice and story to share with the world. How you share that message and story will always be up to you but have the courage to become your number one fan and own PR agent. *And most importantly, stay true to your authentic self while doing so!*

16

The making of choices

By reading this book, you would have now established that each choice you make in life is essentially a choice of one's deep-rooted vibrational intentions. Your vibrational intentions are the compass that gives direction to where your path may lead you in the physical world. If you are consciously aware of all the different parts of yourself, you will always make choices based on the positive emotions you feed yourself. However, if you are not consciously aware of the intentions you keep in your life, you will always make choices based on the feelings that you feed yourself the most, be that good or bad.

You see, what matters when an individual makes a choice is not the choice itself but the emotions one associates with their choices. The deep-rooted intention you hold within yourself and the emotions you associate with will bring you more of what you want or do not want in life.

Let us say in high school, a particular individual severely bullied you. Since high school, you have not seen this individual but come across them later in life. Perhaps years or decades have passed, but you have not forgotten what this individual subjected you to. You have never given them much thought through adulthood, but when you have, you have had feelings of dislike and anger towards them. You may have even gone to the extent of having thoughts of *"getting them back"* if the opportunity were ever to present itself. In adulthood, you have also become a philanthropist and do not hesitate to provide aid or monetary assistance to those in dire need. One day, through your charitable work, you come across a fundraiser to assist an individual in being able to purchase the equipment and drugs they need to help them with their life-saving treatment. Upon further inspection, you realise that the individual who requires treatment is the same individual who bullied you relentlessly in high school. Now the philanthropist and charitable part of you may want to provide the much-needed funds to assist the individual in question. But, if your resentful part is more substantial, you may not wish to offer them any assistance or be torn about what to do due to the mixed emotions you may be feeling. When a person becomes torn between making a choice or decision, they will continuously operate and send out a vibrational intention of confusion and misalignment to the universe, as per our example. As a person's vibrational intentions are here to guide them, one must become consciously aware of the intentions they keep, as it will eventually be reflected in their physical reality, either positively or negatively depending. Suppose a person makes a choice or decision with no conscious awareness of their vibrational intention. In which case, they will always end up wanting or agreeing to something they had no real (pure) intention of adhering to or going along with in the first place. The same individuals will also try to rid themselves of painful experiences, only to find themselves experiencing a similar or if not identical, situation later in life. One may seek to have their life go a certain way, only for it to go the complete opposite way, all because of the unconscious vibrational intentions they hold. Individuals suffering from misalignment will also suffer from feelings of division within themselves, during which they will be in constant battle and left to choose between the two opposing parts of themselves.

To better understand this, one must fathom the concept of unconscious intentions and how this applies to them when they are required to make a choice. There are two parts to an individual's unconscious intentions, *what one gets accustomed to and what one seeks.*

When an individual makes a choice, it is more often than not based on their past behaviours, in other words, what one has grown to become accustomed to and familiar with over time. This familiarity enables the individual to believe they can safely control any external conditions that may have otherwise impacted their choice. Therefore, when they try to follow a new path (what they seek) and make any choices relating to this, they will attempt to break free of their old patterns and the haven of familiarity. Sadly, this is also one of the reasons why many individuals fail. Individuals may experience internal conflicts when seeking a new path and return to what they are accustomed to if they do not become consciously aware of their vibrational intentions.

To ensure a person makes sensible choices that will lead them where they desire to be in life, one must grow familiar with their internal (vibrational) intentions. And as we now know, the only way to do this is to become consciously aware of the intentions we keep. Our vibrational intentions guide us to live the path we seek. Failure to understand this will cause you to make choices that will only create the opposite results of what you truly desire. Therefore, to learn how to cultivate and nourish the needs of your soul, which is the core of your vibrational intentions and being, one should ask themselves the following questions:

- *What is it that I wish to create in this life?*
- *Do the choices I make serve my higher self (vibrational being)? If the answer is no, you are not aligned with their vibrational intentions.*
- *Do I make choices that give me temporary pleasure or lead me to where I desire to be?*

Making an effort to be consciously aware of the vibrational intentions one holds will make it easier to stay on the path that will lead you to one of success and fulfilment. Another technique one can use to guide themselves on their path is to set an intention as soon as one wakes in the morning. One must remember that whatever intention one sets, it ought to fill them with positive, high-flying vibrations like joy, excitement, and happiness. As their day proceeds and one faces various choices, one should repeat the following affirmation to remind themselves of their vibrational intentions:

> *"I am accountable for the choices I make and the aftermath of these choices."*

While a person's choices reflect one's vibrational intentions, an individual who is still learning about being consciously aware of their set intentions can carry conflicting vibrations. Therefore, to prevent these individuals from receiving the results they do not desire, it would be beneficial for them to use the above daily reminder to assist themselves in staying in alignment with the intentions they seek.

The universe has provided us opportunities to evolve to a level of power that ordinary human beings cannot understand. But, by being consciously aware of our decision-making potency, we can enter a new dimension of one's creative capabilities. Enabling oneself to make choices that will align with the greater vibrational intentions of one's soul will carry oneself to heights and blessings one could never have fathomed previously.

That is the power of choice.

17

Visualise your way to success

Visualisation is a valuable tool and creative process that individuals can use to bring into physical form whatever they desire or wish to experience in their lives. It generally works by creating mental images of the things you want to have, own, or experience, combined with the feelings of the positive emotions you would associate with having what it is you desire.

While visualisation usually works with mental images, some can also use the process of visualisation without the use of images. They do this by using the sensations of smell, voice, sound, and taste to get in tune with whatever it is they wish to experience. For example, an individual may want to go on holiday to their dream location. However, while they have never been there in person, by using the process of visualisation they can bring to life the scents or sounds they believe to be associated with the location of their dream holiday.

There is no right or wrong way to visualise. However, it is crucial that you have a positive attitude during the process of visualisation and operate with good feeling emotions, such as joy and bliss. It is also essential to remember that when a person brings something to life using their creative faculties, it has no choice but to come into form in their physical reality, provided the individual truly lives and breathes their visualisations.

It is common knowledge that most athletes also use the practice of visualisation to help them prepare for their future games or matches. These athletes either see themselves as winners or as reaching particular levels of their chosen sport. For example, Arnold Schwarzenegger mentioned numerous times that before he achieved his goals in the physical world, he would first bring them to life in his mind through the power of visualisation. In addition, Michael Jordan, one of the greatest basketball players of all time, has also mentioned numerous times how he used the power of visualisation to become one of the greatest sportsmen in history. Before he achieved the great heights that he did, he first saw it in his mind. There truly is great power in the process of visualisation.

Those who work with and know me well will tell you I am also a keen visualiser. Whenever I want to accomplish or bring to life a specific goal, I first see it in my mind.

I visualise it. Embrace it. Live it. Breathe it.

And yes, it really does work.

I have used the power of visualisation to get pay rises, own luxury items, and have one of my all-time favourite idols feature my first children's book on their channel. Visualisation has brought great things and opportunities into my life, and it can do the same for you.

To visualise, follow the guide below:

1. *Know the definite purpose for your visualisation (what is it that you wish to bring into your physical world and experience)*
2. *Find a quiet spot where you won't be disturbed or distracted.*
3. *Allocate five to ten minutes to complete this exercise (you can also take longer should you wish)*
4. *Choose some calming music (this step is optional, but 777hz music is best should you want to have a relaxing tune in the background)*
5. *Close your eyes*
6. *Do some deep breathing for approximately two to three minutes or longer if needed*
7. *When in a calm state, begin the visualisation process*
8. *Create several collective images in your mind of what it is you wish to be experiencing or achieving, or imagine the sights, sounds, and smells associated with your desire (create a small movie in your mind)*
9. *Feel and connect with the positive emotions of what it would be like if you were experiencing your desire in the physical world*
10. *When ready to end your visualisation, begin to do some deep*

breathing for two to three minutes before opening your eyes again.

When used correctly, the process of visualisation can bring magical experiences and things into a person's life. It can enable the person to vibrate at the same frequency as their greatest desires in life while allowing them to come closer into alignment with what they wish to experience, similar to how affirmations work.

Depending on what you feel comfortable with and what suits your personal needs, some may also wish to combine their visualisation process with a vision board. However, you can also take this process one step further by creating drawings of what it is you want to achieve. Again, you do not have to be an artist to do this, but we recommend taking a drawing book or scrapbook and physically drawing out what you wish to achieve or experience.

For example, if you wish to own a luxury vehicle or live in a large house, draw the image and yourself into it. Now, if you're going to get even more creative, you can also find images of what you desire and photoshop yourself into those images too.

Outlandish? Maybe. Does it work? Yes!

Now, while we don't recommend you share your images with anyone unless you choose to, we do recommend you take a few minutes to stare at the images you have created each day. It would be best if you did this at least twice a day, once in the morning and once at night, for maximum impact. The more a person acts or feels like they are living the experience they seek, the easier it becomes etched in your subconscious mind making it easier for you to receive. But remember, to be able to receive what it is you desire, you must be willing to feel all the wonderful and joyous emotions that one would associate with having or achieving one's greatest goals and desires.

When one harnesses the power of visualisation and sees their dream life and goals complete, they will always accelerate their path to success in the physical world. Moreover, as the visualisation process uses the creative faculties of a person's mind, it motivates them to find the least resistant ways of achieving their dreams and goals, which enables them to shift from a place of self-doubt to that of deep and meaningful growth.

The more a person gets accustomed to the process of visualisation, the more they will find it forms a fundamental part of their thinking process, enabling the individual to come into conscious awareness that they are indeed the creators of their lives. Furthermore, when one's conscious awareness becomes one with their subconscious mind, the individual aligns with their higher self, permitting themselves to let go of their previous programming much more quickly.

You see, most individuals' previous programming involves thinking that they must acquire things or money before achieving their desired success; however, this is not the case. Instead, for an individual to live the life they seek, they must start by connecting to their inner being and definite purpose. One of the most excellent tools for facilitating this is the process of creative visualisation.

Before we end this chapter, we would like to remind you that those who participate in the power of creative visualisation must do so from a sense of prosperity and abundance. This means that you must be consciously aware that what you desire, you will receive. And that the universe will always bring you what your heart and soul genuinely wish. Contrary to what some may tell you, whatever you desire or seek in life is here for the asking. The universe will consistently deliver to you what you are a vibrational match to; this is the law of the universe.

18

Be open to receiving & prosper

When working with individuals, it always amazes me how they always expect the worst in life to happen. The bizarre thing is that most of these so-called terrible life experiences are nothing but a fragment of their imaginations or based on something that happened in the past. Yet, by giving their constant attention to these negative scenarios in their mind, they end up bringing these situations to life and then go, *"See, I told you so,"* or *"I knew this would happen…I have the worst luck in life,"* Which usually compels me to respond with a *"Well, yes, it was bound to happen because you attracted this experience into your life."*

You see, most individuals have learned to expect the worst in life from a young age through the people they spend the majority of time with growing up. Often, this is their parents, guardians, or extended family. But this does not mean one should blame their parents, guardians, or extended family for this type of thinking, as unknown to them, they too have been unconsciously conditioned to expect the worst through the programming that has passed on from one generation to the next.

Thankfully, you are in the position to break this habit of old-style thinking and raise the next generation with full awareness of their magical capabilities to live the life they choose and one filled with prosperity and abundance.

However, a person must be willing to learn and break their old thinking habits while letting go of their scarcity mindset and the fear of constantly expecting the worst to happen in their lives. The more the individual chooses to stay in a scarcity mindset and hold onto worries that the worst is to come, the more they will scrape through life, missing out on the endless opportunities and possibilities available to them to enjoy.

Individuals who commonly suffer from a scarcity mindset are the ones who constantly have thoughts such as:

- *"It is selfish to have more than the next person."*
- *"You have to sacrifice yourself to succeed & prosper."*
- *"There isn't enough money in the world for everyone."*
- *"People out there need money more than I do."*
- *"I would rather be poor than rich."*
- *"Having too much money is bad."*
- *"Money is evil."*

Individuals who choose to have such thoughts do not understand and are not consciously aware of the abundant opportunities the universe can deliver to them. Instead, they hold onto false beliefs based on their lack of understanding of the universe. The universe is here to provide all that we desire in all areas of our lives. All one has to do is ask, have belief in the universe's magic, and be willing to receive it. This is an extremely crucial element in permitting oneself to prosper and shine. Furthermore, this also means that the individual has closed themselves to outside circumstances and no longer allow external conditions such as the news and economic climate to steer them away from receiving the prosperity they crave.

If an individual is constantly doubting they will receive what they are asking for or when it will come into form, then it would be wise for the individual to evaluate their belief system.

To do this, ask yourself the following questions:

- *Can you genuinely see yourself living as a successful, prosperous, fulfilled individual in this life?*
- *Do you feel that prosperity & abundance surround you?*
- *Do you understand & honestly believe that being filled with abundance & prosperity does not take it away from others?*
- *Do you believe you deserve to live a life of success and fulfilment?*

If you answered no to any of the questions we have presented, then it would be safe to assume that your belief system is not one in alignment with that of receiving.

Anytime an individual does not hold strong beliefs about the possibility of being prosperous, they create resistance and block all possible avenues to becoming the best they can be and living a life of success and fulfilment. It is a strange phenomenon, but unless you genuinely believe you deserve success, abundance, and prosperity, you cannot flourish in the manner you wish. It is common for individuals to believe that when they are prosperous and receive all they have asked for, they somehow deprive others of the same opportunities. However, this is not the case. One must understand that being prosperous does not mean that one takes away the prospect for others to be prosperous too.

It is time for individuals to see that receiving what one asks for is not selfish or greedy. Instead, it enables you the opportunity to be of service to others. The more good that comes your way, the more good you can do through the work or services you provide. For example, a common misconception that individuals have are that the wealthy are immoral or greedy. This is not always the case, as many successful individuals in excellent financial positions often provide extensive support to charities or other causes close to their hearts.

Many years ago, when travelling, I had the privilege of experiencing my first business class flight. I remember sitting excitedly on the plane, waiting for the other passengers to board, when a young child who walked past me turned to his father and asked, *"Why are the seats bigger here?"* The father made a point of looking at me as well as the passenger in front of him and me, and then turned to his son and, along with some explicit language, said, *"Because this is where the greedy people sit,"*

While one can argue that everyone is entitled to their opinion, when one makes a statement filled with negative low vibrational feelings, as was with the gentleman on my flight, they open up the gateway to many more undesirable life experiences for themselves. Unfortunately, in this case, not only was the gentleman operating from a place of lack but also one of dislike and jealousy. Unknown to him and others, who make such low vibrational statements, doing so, will only prevent them from living a life of prosperity, abundance, and fulfilment.

If you truly want to live the life you want, you must be open to receiving and willing to accept the best life offers you. This is the only way a person can prosper in the manner they wish. Unfortunately, those who continually struggle with this concept are those with a low self-image of themselves. It is rather sad for individuals to see themselves in such a manner, but one that is all too common in the world.

If you are one of those individuals who struggle, we recommend you carry out 'opinion checks' on yourself throughout the day.

OPINION CHECKS

Opinion checks are asking yourself at different times and situations throughout the day the following questions:

- *"In this current moment, how do I feel about myself?"*
- *"In this current moment, how do I see myself?"*

The purpose of these questions is to give the individual more clarity on the thoughts and images they hold about themselves. One cannot change the opinions one has of themselves unless one takes the time to study and have an in-depth understanding of the low vibrational feelings they have and the causes of this.

Once you overcome your unkind thoughts and negative

image, you will start to create a new vision of yourself and see yourself in a new light, allowing yourself to receive all that you desire and prosper in all areas of your life.

19

The power of healing

Before one tries to exercise the magnificent powers that one holds, it is important to learn to let go and heal from past experiences that have caused you a significant amount of pain.

When an individual chooses to hold onto pain or situations that have brought them misery in the past, they cannot move forward and experience the joys of having a fulfilling life or one blessed with the abundance and prosperity they seek.

All of us, at one time or another in our lives, will go through painful experiences, be that physical or emotional. However, in order to cultivate a new world filled with our greatest desires, we must be willing to rid ourselves of the harmful energy we hold onto because of our past negative experiences. No one can create the life they desire if they continually bring old painful memories to fruition.

It is human nature for individuals unaware of the power of their thoughts and energy to become caught up with constant feelings of *"what should have been"* and *"what ifs"* in life. But unfortunately, such thoughts only provide the perfect conditions to live out our painful memories in the present time repeatedly.

Sure, life is full of twists and turns, but where these twists and turns take you, only you can decide. However, it is certain that those who choose a life filled with abundance and prosperity do not dwell on painful memories. Instead, they work towards healing themselves from past hurt and letting go.

While healing and letting go of painful experiences is vital to begin your journey to fulfilment and success, you must also understand that healing does not mean erasing all the bad and painful experiences from your mind. Rather, it is acknowledging all the negativity that has happened in your lives up until that point but not permitting that negativity to stop you from living your dream life.

A person cannot go through life continually feeding themselves such low vibrational energies and expect to experience the success and abundance they desire in their lives. In order to consciously receive that of which we seek, we must believe that we deserve them and see ourselves as worthy recipients of the beautiful gifts the universe has to offer.

When working with clients who struggle to attract the life experiences they desire, many of them often suffer from a lack of self-worth or feelings of not deserving what they seek. Usually, it is because they feel ashamed or regretful about their past circumstances.

While many circumstances in life may cause a person to feel this way, it is crucial that the individual work towards healing and clearing their energetic blocks.

You see, the energy we put out and vibrate at are the core foundations of being able to create the life we want. But unfortunately, without taking the time to rid ourselves of the excess baggage we carry from our past pain and hurt, we will continually attract more struggle, lack, and unhappiness. But worst of all, we will end up attracting even more pain into our lives to heal from, and no one should want that.

It is sad, but many will go through life carrying within them a giant stockpile of negative emotions, attitudes, and beliefs stemming from nothing but their past negative experiences. It serves no great purpose other than making one spend their lives miserable or trying to escape inner turmoil by attaching themselves to unhealthy habits. These unhealthy habits can range from eating unhealthy foods to staying in a toxic relationship or substance abuse in worst-case scenarios. Furthermore, the physical implications on one's body from carrying such pain and trauma over time is that of illness and disease.

Humans have become so accustomed to holding onto their past trauma and experiences that they worry that by addressing their past pain, they will only amplify the pain and hurt they once experienced. Yet, they spend years and years of their lives reliving painful experiences by having thought after thought of the events that caused them the most hurt.

SURRENDERING & ACCEPTANCE

In order to stop reliving these painful experiences that prevent us from moving forward, we must learn to heal and let go. And the best way to do this is through surrendering and acceptance. Surrendering is the process of freeing oneself from the negative emotions one would associate with a particular event or experience, allowing one to bring into form one's greatest desires in life. Acceptance is the process of recognising what one has faced, acknowledging the pain and hurt, and being consciously aware that these negative past experiences do not form the basis for one's future ventures. With acceptance and surrendering comes harmony with oneself and the opportunity to begin a new journey within your life.

> "Life is one big journey, made up of many small journeys."

The world is beautiful to those who experience the power of healing through surrendering and acceptance. It is the gateway to ridding oneself of past resentments, hurt, and pain, allowing us all to be the creative and vibrational beings we were supposed to be. For you see, when we heal, we no longer fear the future. Instead, we welcome it and embrace the present. As a result, we live in gratitude and no longer greet each waking day with a sense of gloom but rather one of hopefulness.

Of course, there will be times when one surrenders their past experiences, only to find that their feelings of pain and hurt resurface. Do not be alarmed, for it simply means that you have, in fact, not completely healed and require more work in this area. It is important to consider that many individuals spend most of their lives suppressing or ignoring the pain and hurt they feel rather than acknowledging it. Therefore, one cannot undo a lifetime of pain and hurt overnight. Healing takes time. How much time, well, that is dependent on every individual situation. Some go through the healing process at a quicker pace, while others require more time. Whatever the time duration, never compare your healing journey to another, for each of us go through different situations and life experiences. It is important not how long it takes you to go through the healing process but how this process connects you and aligns you with your higher self. When we connect to who we really are, we have a newfound desire to seek out the things that will bring joy and fulfilment to our lives. The benefit of this is that it draws us to great success and prosperity while providing us with a state of calmness within ourselves.

Where there once was a lack of self-worth and regret, there is now self-love and happiness. The beautiful thing about this is that the person who once sought validation or love from others now understands their source of happiness and power is within themselves. The moment this happens, the person begins to abandon any resistance they once had to the endless opportunities that were available to them. This enables them to reach a level that most will not in their lives - knowing that whatever they desire in life will come into form, regardless of their circumstance in the physical world.

"The universe is here to serve all of us, not the other way around."

Epilogue

As our journey together ends, I want to express my gratitude for taking the time to read this book and taking the first steps toward becoming the author of your reality. Just as I have had the pleasure of experiencing beautiful things in my life, you will too.

As I said at the beginning of this book, we all have the capabilities to live a life filled with joy, success, and prosperity. There are endless possibilities available if you take the time to change your thinking patterns, consciously alter your habits and shift your negative thoughts to those that serve your higher self and your definite purpose in life. When a person commits to living a certain way and experiencing joyful life experiences, whatever they desire has no choice but to come into physical form, provided they have rid themselves of their self-limiting and old beliefs.

Without altering your mindset, you cannot read about change and expect results to show up in your life. Change can only happen by doing things differently. Therefore, I have given you several concepts, tools, and exercises throughout this book to assist you in applying these changes to your life to get the desired results you seek.

This book has been crafted through years of experience practising the exercises and tools outlined in this book in my own life and that of my clients. There is nothing in this book I haven't used in my own life that I haven't shared with you.

While you will experience the many benefits of receiving what you desire and living a life of fulfilment, you will also discover that many areas of your life, including how you react to situations, will change. Where you once used to respond with frustration and powerlessness, you will react with love and compassion and learn that no challenge is ever too small or big for you to overcome.

Challenges and failures in life are inevitable, but the important thing is always to remember that with each challenge and failure comes a lesson that guides us to greatness and takes us exactly where we need to go.

The universe will always guide you on the right path, just as it has guided me to write this book and share my work with you. Therefore, it is my desire you take the time to grasp and absorb the concepts described in this book before you begin to exercise your newfound knowledge.

I offer mentoring services if you require extra help and am always available to answer your questions through my website: https://filizbauthor.com/contact/

I wish you all the best in your journey to a better you and a life of fulfilment, and I hope to meet you one day in person, perhaps at one of my seminars or webinars or wherever else our paths may cross in this lifetime. But before I bid you farewell, I want to remind you always to have faith in yourself and your capabilities.

Everything you need to achieve greatness and live a fulfilling life is available to you if you look and unlock the magic within.

Till we meet again –

Acknowledgements

It takes many people to bring a book to life and into the hands of the reader. So, I would like to thank everyone and express my gratitude to those who assisted and supported me along my journey to share this book with you. Your care and support will always be appreciated.

To my friends, thank you for continually listening to me talk about my books and writing and for always offering your undivided attention when doing so. I appreciate each of you.

To my mother and father, who taught me to believe in myself and be whoever I wanted to be in this world, thank you! Your never-ending guidance, love, and support inspire and fill my heart with love each day.

To my brother, thank you for always supporting me in all my endeavours, being my best friend, and always providing the best insights into any situation. I love you dearly.

And to you, the reader, for believing in yourselves and my book, thank you!

Index

A

abundance, 14, 105-106, 110-11
acceptance, 113-114
achievement, 30, 89-90
acting as if, 22-25
affirmation, 11, 29, 32-33, 97
agent
   be your own, 87-92
awareness, 25, 94, 102

B

balance
   find your balance, 58-62
barriers, 19-20, 34
beliefs
   self-limiting beliefs, 19-20, 43-44
blame, 42, 105
boundaries, 60, 64
burnout, 55, 59

C

career, 83
challenges, 89
choices
   the power of choices, 93-97

circumstances, 41-45
confidence, 29-30
   speak with confidence, 55-56
connect, 61-62, 83
control, 42-43

E

energy, 110-111
expectations, 71

F

failure
   embracing failure to succeed, 7-12
fear, 69-73

G

goals, 19, 28, 101-102

H

habits, 46-49
happiness, 75
healing, 73
higher self, 75

I

imagination
   creative imagination, 16-18

J

journaling, 61, 71

L

letting go, 10-11

M

meditation, 61
mentor, 39
mindset
   conquer your mindset, **19-25**
mistakes, **81**
money, 14

N

needs, **53-54**
negotiating, 51
'no'
   the art of saying 'no', **50-57**

P

perfectionism, **80-83**
perseverance, **36-40**
positive
   feelings, **23-24**
pr, **87-92**
purpose
   finding your purpose, **13-18**

R

receiving, **104-109**
relationships, **63-68**
repetition
   the power of repetition, **21-22**
resistance, **25**, 106 - 107, 114
routine, **46-49**

S

self-evaluation, **20-21**
self-love, 114
subconscious mind, **20-21**

success
   comes to those who believe it, **26-30**

V

values
   core values, **84-86**
visualisation
   visualise your way to success, **98-103**

W

willpower, 38

Post pictures or quotes related to this book on social media using the tag **#ElevateBook** so we can like and feature them on our page

ABOUT THE AUTHOR

Filiz Behaettin is an international best-selling author, freelance writer, and speaker based in Australia. A thought leader, she was born and raised in Melbourne and is of Turkish Cypriot heritage. Her unique skill set and experience working in government have enabled Filiz to bring a new perspective to the literature, self-help, and cultural diversity space. A mentor and leader, she is also committed to empowering others, particularly women, to achieve their dreams while equipping them with the tools they need to succeed. Her debut self-help book *Elevate* will allow readers for the very first time to have access to the tools she uses with her clients to enable them to succeed and reach levels they never thought possible.

Along with being active in the self-development arena, Filiz is also the author of the popular children's series *'Henry the Strange Bee,'* making her a strong advocate of children's literature. Her series teaches children to embrace their differences and be whoever they want, regardless of race, colour, or social background. Filiz is available for corporate events and school visits, in person or virtually, and is contactable through her website www.filizbauthor.com

www.ingramcontent.com/pod-product-compliance
Lightning Source LLC
Chambersburg PA
CBHW050316010526
44107CB00055B/2272